DISCONNECT

Disconnect

FACEBOOK'S AFFECTIVE BONDS

Tero Karppi

University of Minnesota Press
Minneapolis
London

The University of Minnesota Press gratefully acknowledges the work of Richard Grusin, editorial consultant, on this project.

A version of "Participate" was previously published as "Happy Accidents: Facebook and the Value of Affect," in *Networked Affect*, ed. Ken Hillis, Susanna Paasonen, and Michael Petit, 221–33 (Cambridge, Mass.: MIT Press, 2015). A version of "Deactivate" was previously published as "Digital Suicide and the Biopolitics of Leaving Facebook," *Transformations*, no. 20 (2011). A version of "Die" was previously published as "Death Proof: On the Biopolitics and Noopolitics of Memorializing Dead Facebook Users," *Culture Machine* 14 (2013): 1–20.

Published by the University of Minnesota Press
111 Third Avenue South, Suite 290
Minneapolis, MN 55401-2520
http://www.upress.umn.edu

The University of Minnesota is an equal-opportunity educator and employer.

Library of Congress Cataloging-in-Publication Data
Karppi, Tero, author.
Disconnect : Facebook's affective bonds / Tero Karppi.
Minneapolis : University of Minnesota Press, [2018] | Includes bibliographical references and index. |
Identifiers: LCCN 2018001582 (print) | ISBN 978-1-5179-0306-0 (hc) | ISBN 978-1-5179-0307-7 (pb)
Subjects: LCSH: Facebook (Electronic resource). | Online social networks. | Affect (Psychology). | Interpersonal relations. | Internet–Social aspects.
Classification: LCC HM743.F33 K37 2018 (print) | DDC 302.30285–dc23
LC record available at https://lccn.loc.gov/2018001582

Contents

Log In

Two billion is the current number of active monthly Facebook users. One trillion is the speculated future value of the social media company, which in 2017 exceeded the $500 billion mark, becoming the fourth most valued company in the tech business. These numbers have value. To begin with, these numbers are the first to indicate how social media have become an important part of our everyday social and cultural practices, and second, they are the first to show how these companies have taken their share of our attention, monetized our social relations, and established a position in the stock market. While these are the two sides of social media, their story is often fabulated through the former. To exemplify, the story of connected users is highlighted in Facebook's mission to give people the power to share and make the world more open and connected. In its recently revised mission statement, the company underlines that the value of Facebook is in how it is changing and shaping the world in which we live, by giving "people the power to build community and bring the world closer together."[1] The world connected by Facebook is seen as something for which we should actively strive. According to Mark Zuckerberg, the face, founder, and CEO of Facebook:

> there is a huge need and a huge opportunity to get everyone in the world connected, to give everyone a voice and to help transform society for the future. The scale of the technology and infrastructure that must be built is unprecedented, and we believe this is the most important problem we can focus on.[2]

Connectivity, these discourses try to prove, is the cultural logic of how people and things are bonded with each other and how the societies of the future will operate. For the past decade, not only social media companies but also social media studies and the analyses of connectivity have bought into this view of connectivity and intensely focused on individual and collective user participation enabled by the different platforms. The notion that social media can give voice to the unheard and solve large societal problems stems from these studies, which often frame users as rational subjects and place faith in the possibilities of democratic participation enabled by Facebook, Twitter, and the like. We are often so lured by the narratives of active social media users that the economic value of ubiquitous connectivity and the conditions that produce user subjectivities remain in the shadows. For if the "goal of connectivity is to make everyone and everything part of a single world," as Andrew Culp points out,[3] then for social media companies seizing the opportunity, the potential for world building is also a possibility for a redistribution of wealth and accumulation of capital. From the perspective of money, our social media connections are not neutral, social media connectivity is artificial rather than natural, and the world connected is actively produced and shaped for profit.

The project of this book is to unbind the bonds that make social media connectivity. To do this, the book focuses on what is immanent to every connection: disconnection. There is no connection without disconnection, as Ben Light tells us in *Disconnecting with Social Networking Sites*.[4] Every connection is accompanied by disconnection as a potentiality. Often, the value of each connection is measured against disconnection; some connections are seen as necessary, others as random. But disconnections, per se, are important and even elemental. Disconnections, in our network culture, take different forms: a break, a manifesto, an act, a form of resistance, a failure. They express the vulnerabilities of social media and bring us to the volatility of social media business models based on establishing, enabling, and sustaining connectivity.

Disconnect examines how disconnections work and function and who they work and function for—positioning the problem as such, I am paraphrasing Gilles Deleuze and Félix Guattari, who argue against forcing things into a single essence or real meaning and for moving attention to "intensities, flows, processes, and partial objects."[5] Thus the question of disconnection is a question of how much, how, and in what cases does it appear rather than what it is.[6] With this approach, what can be avoided are the simplified reductions of disconnections into binaries. To disconnect is not exclusively to opt out, leave social media platforms, pull the plug, turn down power, unfriend, commit digital suicide, or take a digital detox and return to a life without social media. These phenomena do not explain what disconnection is but explicate where it becomes operational and how it connects to our understanding of social media. To paraphrase Tiziana Terranova, taking such an approach is "to think *simultaneously* the singular and the multiple, the common and the unique."[7]

The work of disconnection is to trespass into the culture of connectivity and do violence to the dominant image of thought.[8] To disconnect is to open different ways of thinking our engagements with social media platforms. It seems we cannot get rid of binaries completely; for example, from the perspective of participation, disconnection sets a spectrum where questions of use stand on one end and those of nonuse on the other.[9] Inspired and in some cases, perhaps, dazzled by the possibilities of the former, what have stayed largely out of focus in scholarly research are the problems of the latter: disruptions, accidents, disengagements, and disconnects that accompany digital networks. And yet these moments of disconnection, as Light has argued, shape the ways in which we experience social media sites and make them work for us.[10] Light sees disconnection as a solution addressed by individuals to different problems of living with social media. We "cannot be connected to everything all the time," and "therefore we have to disconnect in some way in order to make the connections we want to emphasize at a particular point in time feasible," he elucidates.[11]

Light's active user, who disconnects with social media, is what Amanda Lagerkvist describes as an existential subject of digital culture who "is imbricated in socio-technological ensembles, traversing these terrains more or less successfully, in search for what may be cautiously termed existential security."[12] Let us begin with three stories of disconnection with social media that we often witness circulating online, stories that give us a view to the complexity of the issue at hand from the perspectives of everyday users and their participation. The first story is about individuals.

"The rules of Camp Grounded were simple: no phones, computers, tablets or watches; work talk, discussion of people's ages and use of real names were prohibited," argues Matt Haber, one of three hundred participants who paid $300 to voluntarily abandon their iPhones, laptops, and social media sites for three days at Camp Grounded, organized by the Digital Detox movement.[13] Camp Grounded is one of the places where you can go when the world technologically connected becomes overwhelming and you need a break. It offers you buyout from a situation that you have most likely voluntarily accepted by signing up on a number of social media sites and purchasing a smartphone, which keeps you connected to these networks regardless of your physical location or time zone. "Disconnect to reconnect" is the slogan of the movement, and according to Haber,

> by removing the things that supposedly "connect" us in this
> wireless, oversharing, humble-bragging age, the founders of Digital
> Detox hoped to build real connections that run deeper than
> following one another on Twitter or "liking" someone's photo on
> Instagram.[14]

The idea of digital detox is to connect people without technological mediators and draws on the trope that the online connections are not authentic in the same sense as face-to-face contacts with other people. By removing technologically mediated connections, the campaign helps us to perceive the role and significance these technologies have in our lives. Indeed, Camp Grounded is one example of the constant resistance against being connected to social media sites. Private individuals, media theorists, and lifestyle gurus alike voice this resistance; to disconnect is to reclaim real life, whatever that is. For others, the reasons to quit can be more rationally defined; social media sites violate individual privacy, exploit user information for marketing purposes, harm so-called real-life relationships, or disturb their productivity by constantly interrupting their processes. In all of these voices, social media have become a dominating nuisance interfering in our lives at multiple levels at home, in the office, and in relationships both private and public.

The second story is about the body and the brain, and it also starts with the voice of Camp Grounded visitor Haber:

> There was a phantom buzzing in my shorts. I had carried my
> iPhone in my left front pocket for so many years that my jeans

have permanent rectangular fade marks over my thigh. By now the phone is almost an extension of my nervous system; even without the thing on my person, I could still feel it tingle like a missing limb.[15]

Phantom vibration is a condition where individuals are so connected with their mobile phones that they occasionally experience them vibrating even if the phone is not with them. The sensations are said to resemble the feelings of people whose body parts have been amputated.[16] So connected we are with our devices that provide us constant messages and tweets from the surrounding world that they have become part of our bodies. We are not only using social media technologies but living together with them. In this technopathological condition of what Mark Deuze calls "media life,"[17] our "brains and bodies," as Tony D. Sampson notes, "are in constant processual exchanges with their sensory environments."[18] We live in and with media, and they impact our lives in different ways. These ways cannot be reduced only to our social contacts with each other but sometimes, as in the case of phantom vibrations, they affect the body as whole. Sampson points out that social media sites such as Facebook are sensory terrains where the body and the brain are susceptible to being triggered and captured beyond cognitive preferences at the level of neurotransmitters.[19] There is also a more general concern with the connection of the brain and social media. For example, in a *New York Times* article about the negative impact of social media for our professional careers, Cal Newport notes that "social media weakens" the ability to concentrate without distraction, "because it is designed to be addictive," and the more you use social media, the more the "brain learns to crave a quick hit of stimulus at the slightest hint of boredom."[20] This is a concern of attention and the cognitive capacity to act in this world degenerated by social media use: the brain needs downtime. Being always online changes us and affects on our capacity to act.[21] As such, social media turn us brainless; if we do not disconnect, we are in jeopardy of becoming phantoms vibrating according to the notifications of our social media connections. Disconnection is no longer contextualized as a choice of luxury but has become an issue of health and an individual responsibility.

The third story is about collectives. The visitors to Camp Grounded do not belong to any particular demographic group, even though Laura Portwood-Stacer has noted that disconnecting social media demands affinities such as social capital.[22] And yet, groups and collectives are seen to flee social media sites. The first official Quit Facebook Day was organized for May 31, 2010, gathering more than thirty thousand participants. Different demographic groups, such as teens, are often noted to leave dominant social media platforms like Facebook or Twitter and move to new alternatives. Instagram, the photo-sharing site, is capturing users with its visual approach. Snapchat and the ephemerality of messages that disappear after a while are grasping the pace of mundane, everyday communication. Yik Yak provides anonymity for opinions, yet builds communities based on location. These social media sites adhere to the ideological and technological foundations of the Web 2.0 business models that began at the turn of the new millennium and were built around users and their participatory online practices. As José van Dijck argued, this is the moment when online activities like microblogging, videoconferencing, and photo and video sharing were introduced to a larger audience but were also commodified and branded by particular companies, such as Blogger, YouTube, and Flickr.[23] It is also a time when online shopping with companies like eBay and Amazon started to challenge traditional retailers and when Wikipedia made composing and updating dictionaries a voluntary and participatory activity by a community of users dispersed by time and space. These sites relied on users' content production and mode of participation, which was highlighted by the business ideology of Web 2.0, but equally important was the number of active users. The sites that were able to capture masses of users survived and beat their competition. For example, Twitter, notably the most famous and successful microblogging site, was challenged by a number of sites offering similar services, such as Jaiku, which Google bought in 2007 and shut down in 2012,[24] after reports of users fleeing to Twitter.[25] There is and has been an ecology of different social media platforms fighting for users' participation and demanding their presence. In this third story, disconnection is no longer about you and me but about masses of users moving between social media platforms and the services they offer.

The three preceding stories address the different bonds users form with social media and through social media. Disconnection is seen as a solution either to the problems of particular connections or to a general state of being always connected and letting social media dominate users' lives. As a form of a solution, disconnection is seen as a way out.

The argument of this book, however, demands that we temporarily forget what disconnection means for users and position it as a problem for social media platforms. If disconnection is a solution for some social media users, for the social media platforms and their shareholders, it becomes an existential crisis. Social media live and breathe their users. Users are their asset and user engagement forms a bond almost in a financial sense; it allows the platform to function but it also means that the platform is highly dependent on its users and the engagements they make. As Facebook stated:

> if we are unable to maintain or increase our user base and user engagement, our revenue and financial results may be adversely affected. Any decrease in user retention, growth, or engagement could render our products less attractive to users, marketers, and developers, which is likely to have a material and adverse impact on our revenue, business, financial condition, and results of operations.[26]

For social media platforms, disconnection is a problem of control, governance, and design. It is a problem of how to keep users engaged with the platform—how to integrate and control the circulation of users, links, and nodes—but also a problem of keeping value, attention, and desires within the system.

This problem is the focus of *Disconnect*. It finds its stories where the human user is no longer the *primus motor* of social media connections. It focuses on moments where connectivity is in a constant stage of crisis, contested by disconnection, and this potential threat gives social platforms their justification to build new engagements. As Light and Elijah Cassidy note, "Disconnection does not necessarily corrupt Facebook's desires and need for user connections; conversely, it is integral to it. . . . Facebook keeps users in their place and suppresses conflicts so that money can be made."[27] This positioning of disconnection as a productive force bears a resemblance to how Wendy Hui Kyong

Chun talks about crises as turning points that drive system updates and software changes,[28] but with a stronger emphasis on the futurity of crisis. In other words, disconnection is there, but in the form of a threat rather than anything actual. To position disconnection as a threat is to say that it is virtual. Disconnection is always present as a virtual against which the actual unfolds. Disconnection is threat in a productive form. This threat engineers our connectivity[29] and programs our sociality,[30] to use van Dijck's and Bucher's terms. To prepare for disconnection is to anticipate that it will happen, establish possible scenarios of prevention, and let these scenarios impact the present.

Here disconnection opens a spectrum where users are on one end and the platform is on the other. In other words, explaining social media by looking for users' experiences of connections and disconnections, coloring a bright picture of user participation, or addressing the many benefits of interacting with each other on social media sites is no longer central. In contrast, forging ahead is the capacity of social media to modulate their users based on data, affective contagions, and the sociotechnological conditions of the platforms. The social media user is in a particular position within a system that has the capacity to affect its agency and assign it with a particular identity.

What follows from the perspective of disconnection is a contestation of how we are used to defining the social media user. The rationally participating actor who decides to disconnect and the individual who is emotionally drawn into the feedback loops of the system and hence too addicted to disconnect are given a third alternative. Disconnecting "from the tyranny of social media," as Grant Bollmer puts it, does not help us to discover a "'true' human nature" but helps us to think how our being is "an effect of the ways we use and describe technology."[31] The social media user, caught between connections and disconnections, resembles Deleuze's *dividual,* a much-repeated idea that individuals are split into offline and online presences.[32] What bonds these two sides is of interest here. The user is located somewhere in the split, affected and subjectified by both sides. What manifests between the online and offline presence is an idea of "mesmerized subjectivity," as described by Sampson through the social theory of Gabriel Tarde, a sociologist, criminologist, and social psychologist of the late 1800s; this user functions somewhere between inseparability and insensibility of "mechanical habit and dream of volition."[33] This user uses social media in her own individual purposes and is engaged with a larger social whole but is also captured and modulated by the social media platforms through profiling, predictive analytics, and suggestive algorithms, to name a few examples.[34]

To approach the social media users through their engagements and affective bonds produced, conditioned, and modulated by the platform often means painting with a pallet of shades of gray. What are highlighted are the negative sides of user engagement; users are an essential part of the system, but they are also becoming increasingly defined by the system itself. When social media users log in on social media, agency is given to the nonhuman. To be a little less figurative, if media theory has been traditionally divided into phenomenological and material approaches, this work finds its allies in the context of the latter.[35]

Hence this book is part of what could be defined as the nonhuman turn of social media studies, aligning with but not exclusively retaining emerging and evolving fields like platform studies or studies of software cultures.[36] The role of the human is still important in these nonhuman approaches, but rather than starting from the individual, they are mapping the complex technosocial fabric that conditions our possibilities and building a context where being a human occurs and takes shape. One of the predecessors of this line of thinking is Friedrich Kittler, with his attempts to decentralize the human perspective and his argument that media are not extensions or prostheses of a human being but what override our sensory capabilities.[37] The human in Kittler's line of thinking, as, for example, Geoffrey Winthrop-Young points out, is merely one node among others whose agency is both restricted and enabled by the network where she connects.[38] Kittler has been accused of having a negative and even inhuman understanding of our technological relations, where "the human element increasingly disappears as technology . . . works its way toward complete, inhuman autonomy."[39] Central to Kittler's argument, however, is not so much the suggested deterministic teleology as the observation that the materiality of a given medium matters beyond its physicality and as such also conditions human existence. "The dominant information technologies of the day control all understanding and its illusion," Kittler states.[40] This epistemological claim dispositions understanding as a form of agency that is neither entirely human nor nonhuman but something that happens in between. Therefore an activity such as thinking never happens in isolation but always in encounters with the world. "There is something in the world that forces us to think," Deleuze famously argues.[41] This is a notion of both control and resistance: the established conditions that try to force thinking into a particular mold also liberate forces to think against them.[42]

The materiality argument can also be used to refute the notion that software is immaterial and move the perspective to how these systems are operative in this world.[43] For example, Chun argues that not only are digital interfaces and operating systems tools to access and use computer hardware but they are also shaping our practices, individualizing our experiences, and eventually producing us as "users" in and with the system.[44] "Software is functional in nature," as Alexander Galloway puts it.[45] While the importance of software is often highlighted in these earlier studies, the current relocation of the issue to the level of the social media platform opens a wider spectrum of nonhuman agencies involved. Platforms are more than the software. According to Carolin Gerlitz, "platforms are technical infrastructures involved in data production and processing."[46] Tarleton Gillespie takes this notion a step further, noting that "platforms are socio-technical assemblages and complex institutions."[47] Social media platforms, taken as complex assemblages, are composed of software and hardware but also things such as policies, terms of service, and business models, which are all "cultural techniques"[48] with unique capacities to act and particular user models to impose. Hence to turn the perspective to the nonhuman means also focusing on users beyond their individuality and sociality. Following the train of thought of Sampson and Chun, the social in social media is a relation that is constantly produced through establishing and modulating not only user practices but also collective conditions for attraction, habit, and other modes of coming together.[49] In this framework, neither the human who becomes and interacts with the system nor the system, online network, or social media platform where we operate should be taken as given. Rather, the relations between the two should be seen as actively forming, taking place in various affective encounters.[50] What is tracked, then, is not so much how we made media social but how social media sites condition the ways in which we can have cultural practices, such as sociality, participation, sharing, or content production, and also how our cognitive capacities are captured and modulated on these platforms at the level of affective flow.[51]

Follow the Money

Facebook the social networking service and social media platform is also Facebook Inc., a social media business. On March 12, 2018, one share of Facebook stock can be purchased for approximately $184.97. Facebook has a market capitalization of $537.50 billion and generated $40 billion in revenue in 2017. As a business, Facebook relies on users and cannot survive without their connections. In this book, attention is given to the critical analysis of the economic value of social media platforms and the relations they encompass. To rephrase, the interest is in social media platforms in the two senses of the word *platform*: as a sociotechnological system and as a mechanism of producing, distributing, and managing economic relations. Provocative predictions of the death of Facebook due to disconnection circulate around these two takes on *platform,* and the threat of users leaving the site finds its literal manifestations in the financial documents of publicly traded social media companies.[52] When Facebook in 2012 became a publicly traded company, it openly admitted that its challenge is to keep growing and maintain the existing user base.[53] When Twitter informed that it had lost two million users in the last three months of 2015, newspapers reported that its share price dropped 12 percent.[54] The value of these sites relies on users, not necessarily as active agents, but as numbers that fit into the metrics of success.

Social media metrics, such as the constant measurement of monthly active users, and how these numbers affect stock prices underline the fact that social media is a business. Social media sites render relationships calculable, and as David Beer notes, this rendering is interwoven with new cultural understandings and ideological changes, for example, to update one's life on sites like Facebook is to accept their definitions of privacy.[55] Relations on social media sites are not only connections between people; they also serve as data aggregates and bait to draw users' attention.[56]

The companies, however, as Yuval Dror maintains, often downplay the business side.[57] For example, in his letter to investors, Zuckerberg underlines that "Facebook was not originally created to be a company.

It was built to accomplish a social mission—to make the world more open and connected."[58] Yet the way he continues this description implies that making the world more open and connected has become a part of Facebook's business: "We think it's important that everyone who invests in Facebook understands what this mission means to us, how we make decisions and why we do the things we do."[59] Similarly, the letter to investors by @Twitter, not the CEO, highlights how the site has grown from a service "shaped by the people for the people" into a business:

> The mission we serve as Twitter, Inc. is to give everyone the power
> to create and share ideas and information instantly without
> barriers. Our business and revenue will always follow that mission
> in ways that improve—and do not detract from—a free and global
> conversation.[60]

Revenue may be the side product of the social mission, but social media sites do have exact mechanisms of monetization. Beverly Skeggs and Simon Yuill have analyzed the sources of Facebook's finances and categorized them into four different operations. First, Facebook is capital. You can buy Facebook on the stock market. Second, Facebook is not capital intensive, and its starter costs and fixed costs are low. Third, advertising revenue, which directly targets users and their relationships, is the major source of revenue for Facebook, which, as Skeggs and Yuill note, accounted for 82 to 85 percent of Facebook profits. Fourth, Facebook has implemented things like "Promoted Posts," in-game purchases, transaction costs, and gifts and deals within its platform. According to Skeggs and Yuill, Facebook possesses "adaptability," "computing power," and "monopoly control"; it is able to capture other sites and services and financialize and monetize even further.[61]

Indeed, the social media sites that thrive seem able not only to capture users but also to expand their business to the fabric of users' everyday lives. This is exemplified again by their mission to make the world connected and give everyone the power to create and share. They are producing a world where social media are pervasive and ubiquitous. As the *Facebook Annual Report 2015* declares:

> our top priority is to build useful and engaging products that
> enable people to connect and share through mobile devices and

personal computers. We also help people discover and learn about what is going on in the world around them, enable people to share their opinions, ideas, photos and videos, and other activities with audiences ranging from their closest friends to the public at large, and stay connected everywhere by accessing our products.[62]

A similar ethos, which relates user engagement to the pervasiveness and ubiquity of social media in our everyday lives, can be also seen in Twitter's *Annual Report 2016*:

> Twitter gives everyone the power to create and share ideas and information instantly without barriers. Our service is live—live commentary, live connections, live conversations. Whether it is breaking news, entertainment, sports, or everyday topics, hearing about and watching a live event unfold is the fastest way to understand the power of Twitter. Twitter has always been considered a "second screen" for what is happening in the world and we believe we can become the first screen for everything that is happening now. And by doing so, we believe we can build the planet's largest daily connected audience.[63]

The pervasiveness of social media in our everyday lives produces a state where the problem is not how to get connected but how to disconnect. Paraphrasing Steven Shaviro, "no matter what position you seek to occupy, that position will be located somewhere on the network's grid."[64]

Data Power

Helen Kennedy and Giles Moss call the techniques of producing, mining, and analyzing social media relations "data power."[65] The context described in *Disconnect* is a context where data power conditions the possibilities on the network's grid. Data power is seen as a mode of power that is not repressive but seductive and inviting. As Michel Foucault notes,

> what makes power hold good, what makes it accepted, is simply the fact that it doesn't only weigh on us as a force that says no, but that it traverses and produces things, it induces pleasure, forms knowledge, produces discourse. It needs to be considered as a

productive network which runs through the whole social body, much more than as a negative instance whose function is repression.[66]

Within these parameters, power takes two forms: disciplinary power, where the actions of individual bodies are trained, and biopower, where the movements of masses of people are modulated.[67] Both forms of power are alive and well on social media platforms.

Data in data power represents not only the power of information or knowledge but more widely the operationalization of data and their uses in our current culture. Whatever we do on social media platforms, one thing is evident: our actions produce data. These data are not just information about our likes and preferences but build the groundwork for modulation of users, their identities, and their interests, as Ganaele Langlois maintains.[68] In fact, neither these data nor the platform involved in their production is neutral or objective. Different techniques, technologies, and practices of mining, interpreting, and implementing data are also always influencing them, as danah boyd and Kate Crawford argue.[69] Things are also left out. As Nancy K. Baym proposes, instead of falling into the illusions of big data, we should ask ourselves, "what data are not seen, and what cannot be measured?"[70] While data are used in decision making, designing new platform features, or selling ads, they never give the whole picture or stand as a truth but yet have an impact that becomes real.

According to José van Dijck, we live in a *culture of connectivity*, which emanates from a situation where "engineers found ways to code information into algorithms that helped brand a particular form of online sociality and make it profitable in online markets—serving a global market of social networking and user-generated content."[71] She argues that perhaps we should replace the term *social media* with *connective media*, because the use of social rhetoric hides the sociotechnic and politicoeconomic aspects of these platforms.[72] Talking about connective media would for her move the focus toward the platform architecture and how it works as an assemblage of power by making different kinds of connections and transforming these connections into streams of data. Whichever term we choose, social media platforms have power to "influence human interaction on an individual and community level, as well as a large societal level."[73]

As an example, one can refer to the discussions surrounding the U.S. presidential elections of 2016. In this election, social media had an important role in distributing the news. The problem was that what circulated on social media platforms was not only news from fact-checked media outlets but also fake news created to influence opinions, generate revenues through advertising mechanisms, or simply create cognitive dissonance. Zuckerberg responded to the criticism of fake news on his Facebook status, saying, "Identifying 'truth' is complicated." He continued that Facebook's goal is "to give every person a voice" and implicated that it is succeeding, since "of all the content on Facebook, more than 99% of what people see is authentic. Only a very small amount is fake news and hoaxes."[74]

In the same status update, the first comment that is visible is by a Facebook user, who responds to Zuckerberg by claiming:

> If you really believe your statement "Of all the content on Facebook, more than 99% of what people see is authentic." Then you haven't been reading the same newsfeed I have. There's a helluva lot more FAKE and INCORRECT junk on my newfeed [sic] than 1%.[75]

The problem of fake news is not so much what is seen as how things become visible on the platform in the first place. Zuckerberg, in his response, affirms this point: "The stat I mentioned is across the whole system. Depending on which pages you personally follow and who your friends are, you may see more or less. The power of Facebook is that you control what you see by who you choose to connect with."[76] Ironically, the highlighted visibility of this Facebook user's comment already shows how Facebook's mechanisms select meaningful content; this comment appears first not because it is the first or the newest comment on that thread but because it is defined as meaningful by the platform most likely because of the number of responses it and its response have received. As evidenced by the discussion between Zuckerberg and this Facebook user, the neutrality of the platform is a question not only of content shared and circulating on the platform but also of the operations that manage that content on the platform. In fact, in the aforementioned status update, Zuckerberg identifies a second goal for Facebook: "to show people the content they will find most meaningful."[77]

Important here is that what is defined as "meaningful" for users is produced by a plethora of different nonhuman agencies operating alongside the human user on social media platforms.[78] This production is taking place both on the audiovisual interface and under the hood, coded in the software and inscribed in protocols, rules, and regulations. First, what is determined to be meaningful is composed of probabilities and statistical calculations based on user data. To return to the example of the U.S. presidential elections, consider one player in the game: Cambridge Analytica. After the election, the *New York Times* ran a story on its opinion pages about this company being hired by the Trump campaign.[79] Cambridge Analytica, according to the company website, uses "data modeling and psychographic profiling to grow audiences, identify key influencers, and connect with people in ways that move them to action."[80] The news story mentions that the company was using Facebook as a tool to build psychological profiles of more than two hundred million adult Americans and has up to five thousand data points on each individual; some of these data points are from the records of local and state governments, but some were generated by users' behaviors on social media and, for example, answers to "personality quizzes floating around Facebook."[81] While the role of Cambridge Analytica in the elections has been contested, this example still illustrates how complex the data relations are seen and what they potentially could enable.[82]

Targeted marketing is just one example of a place where we see social media using the data we provide to profile us and surround us with "meaningful" content. Taina Bucher's work on Facebook's EdgeRank algorithm shows how these sites constantly engineer our relations.[83] As Bucher notes, the Facebook News Feed controlled by the algorithm has two different versions: top news and most recent news. While most recent news items appear in the order of posting, the top news items are curated by the most interesting content. What is most interesting or meaningful? The answer for each user is produced by Facebook's EdgeRank algorithm. According to this algorithm, the meaningfulness of the content you see is based on information about the people on the platform with whom you interact the most. Other factors, such as number of likes and comments and the pace of affective responses, also matter. Social media profile us and anticipate our interests by design.

Algorithms such as EdgeRank or Google's PageRank, which determines search results, are generative rules, "virtuals that generate a whole variety of actuals."[84] We do not see the algorithm in operation, but we do see its results in the choices and limitations given to us. If the algorithm works well, we receive suggestions regarding things that we are interested in already or things that we might become interested in eventually. If it doesn't work well, we become trapped in an echo chamber of our own and our friends' former likes, clicks, and other interactions. As Bernhard Rieder in his analysis of PageRank points out, these systems "produce specific social consequences themselves."[85] The negative social consequences, the echo chamber, are often called the "filter bubble," a state where users are trapped in the loop of their past interactions with the platform.[86]

Data mining combined with algorithmic control is an example of data power. Users surrender to this power when they sign up for social media accounts. The meaningful things circulating on social media guided by the informational and structural power of the platform do not only appeal to the rational subject. They are also emotional or affective. In politics, we have seen discussions where rational-choice models have given way to more affect-based approaches, which argue that emotions like fear and anger are important factors in guiding voting behaviors.[87] As R. Kelly Garret in his column published in *The Conversation* implies, when we combine anger with the filter bubble, we begin to understand the real power of social media platforms.[88] To articulate Facebook as a platform of emotional contagion, Garrett draws on Facebook's study called "Experimental Evidence of Massive-Scale Emotional Contagion through Social Networks." In this study, researchers "manipulated the extent to which people ($N = 689,003$) were exposed to emotional expressions in their News Feed."[89] These experiments concluded,

> For people who had positive content reduced in their News Feed, a larger percentage of words in people's status updates were negative and a smaller percentage were positive. When negativity was reduced, the opposite pattern occurred. These results suggest that the emotions expressed by friends, via online social networks, influence our own moods.[90]

By inviting, seducing, and activating people, social media produces both emotional and rational subjects and subjectivities. According to this experiment, social media engagements provide a "perfect test bed, or nursery," as Sampson puts it, for user manipulation, attention capture, and emotional suggestion.[91]

Facebook's emotional contagion experiment sheds light on the non-subjective and impersonal forces of nonhuman social media. In their encounters with the social media platform's experiments, users were reduced to bodies with the capability to affect and become affected, and their "individual intention and agency" were captured by what Susanna Paasonen, Ken Hillis, and Michael Petit call "entanglement in technological networks of transmission and communication."[92] Non-human studies of social media here enter the realm of affect theory, where affect is "evoked as an active, contingent dynamic or relation that orients interpretation and moves readers, viewers, and listeners in very physical ways," as Paasonen et al. maintain.[93] Affect is set somewhere between activity and passivity. This notion of affect is central to this book, and it is indebted to Brian Massumi's definition of the concept, which follows in Spinoza's footsteps:

> Spinoza's ethics in the philosophy of the becoming-active, in parallel, of mind and body, from an origin in passion, in impingement, in so pure and productive a receptivity that it can only be conceived as a third state, an excluded middle, prior to the distinction between activity and passivity: affect.[94]

On social media, it is affect that sets things into motion. Affect relies not only on human bodies, on different social media users, but also on nonhuman bodies, such as like buttons, gifs, and recommendation algorithms, which orient the ways in which relations can unfold. For Sampson, who again follows Tarde, the human and nonhuman encounters are based on microrelations that take place below the "cognitive awareness of social association."[95] Affect triggers us and them and puts things into action. Affect matters, and matter affects. Thus social media platforms are always both similar and different. They set up a field of intensity where affect works and manifests in platform-specific activities and bonds: clicks, likes, comments, tweets, event invitations, data relations, and shared experiences of belonging to something. To understand data power, one needs to understand not only data but affect and how affect and data on these platforms are used to condition our being at the limits of our experiences, ideas, and processes of knowledge production.

Culture of Disconnectivity

Disconnect examines social media relations through what challenges and transforms them. Disconnection is an affective force the intensity of which the platform must acknowledge. In this study, my focus is on the affective bonds of one specific social media platform: Facebook. Facebook has redefined how we understand social media first as a website, then as a platform, and currently as a business. Facebook has gone through notable changes from being the face book for Harvard students, connecting people in different parts of the world, becoming a publicly traded company, and taking a market share comparable to Apple, Alphabet, and Microsoft. Facebook is not the first or the last social media platform whose success has been built on users and their relations, but it is the social media platform often referred to when issues of disconnection arise in media and popular culture. If we think about the scale of operation and pervasiveness of particular social media sites, Facebook, with two billion users, is the biggest and most impressive social media platform to date. For its users, Facebook is a medium that has more than instrumental value. Richard Grusin has argued that, "although media and media technologies have operated and continue to operate epistemologically as modes of knowledge production, they also function technically, bodily, and materially to generate and modulate individual and collective affective moods or structures of feeling among assemblages of humans and non humans."[96] For the two billion users, Facebook is a medium that, at least ephemerally, becomes a socially realized structure of engagement where particular social and cultural practices, technological limits, and ontological and epistemological capabilities are shared and negotiated every time we check for new notifications, post status updates, or use Facebook Messenger to send money to our friends. The possibility to disconnect from Facebook is a question that exceeds nonuse and enters the regimes of social and affective power, knowledge production, and cultural practices.

I have been collecting and examining the research materials for *Disconnect* for roughly seven years. Facebook's initial public offering on

Friday, May 18, 2012, for this book is the turning point, which denotes a new epoch for social media. Many of the materials examined in this book emerge around that time and in conjunction with how the company, its interface, and its business models transform. This epoch is characterized by social media becoming a business, and the bonds we have are not only social but also economic. Being a publicly traded company, Facebook is a business that relies on its users and the connections they have. The company's success addresses its capability to sustain the platform; capture and fulfill users' needs and desires; and adapt to changing political, cultural, and technological landscapes. The threat of disconnection is and has been an issue that is part of the platform's future prospective and business plans—perhaps not directly, but it looms in the background as something that is anticipated, preempted, and prepared for. The subsequent positioning of the user in a network of data power, governance, and control, as examined in this book, is not only particular to Facebook but also general to most of the social media sites that aim at being a successful business.

To examine disconnections in this context is to look at online connections and connectivity from multiple angles.[97] Van Dijck argues that the sociocultural understanding of Facebook requires that we look into its interface, protocols, and metadata but also include its business models and legal terms of use in our analysis.[98] I have tried to follow this proposition to produce a well-situated understanding of the meaning of disconnection for Facebook. The research materials used in this book can be divided into two categories. The first category includes Facebook-related texts and discourses and visual interfaces, protocols, and software applications that situate and condition users with the platform. These materials include Facebook's marketing materials; financial documents; documents that describe rules, regulations, and policies; documents that describe investor relations; help desk advice; FAQ texts; developer documents; blog posts; journalistic texts; interviews; and technical specifications of the particular platform, in addition to descriptions of algorithms and their functions. The latter category includes different social media software–related applications, such as tactical media projects and art projects; consumer smartphone applications; and technological applications, such as devices used to access social media sites. These materials position social media as a technical, social, and economic system of governance, organization, and control.

The different chapters of this book are built on a proposition that a way to map, trace, and contest these structures and processes of social media is to look at the moments where it breaks, becomes challenged, and is vulnerable. What is broken, challenged, and vulnerable is the relation of engagement, the bond, between users and the platform. The idea that we bond with social media is given in this context, but how we bond indicates that there are specific manifestations that change through time.[99] That is, bonding does not explain anything, but it needs to be explained as a platform-specific relation. What it means to be bonded and engaged with Facebook, in this book, is a question of Foucault's biopolitics to the extent that it deals with the governmentality and control of the (media) life of Facebook users through the conditions of the platform (chapters 1 and 3–5). The development and redesigns of the platform focus on keeping the users engaged (chapters 1 and 2). The security user engagement establishes is crucial for the platform's business success, as indicated by a number of Facebook's financial reports, which state disconnection as a major risk for its existence (chapter 1). User engagement enables the circulation of data, affect, and value. Facebook's bonds are affective. This does not mean that they are emotion based; emotion is affect captured. Affect precedes emotions, like it precedes the formations of individuals and collectives. Massumi says that affect is "pure sociality," that it is "ready to become all manner of social forms and contents."[100] When Facebook establishes an infrastructure that keeps users engaged (chapter 2), it does so by conditioning affect and setting up parameters for transindividual levels of becoming individuals, users, and collectives. The bonds aim to harness what Massumi calls affect's "active pressure towards taking-form," the openness of being affected.[101] From this perspective, engagement establishes a relation of governance and control as modulation. Modulation, as Deleuze defines it, is "a self-deforming cast that will continuously change from one moment to the other, or like a sieve whose mesh will transmute from point to point."[102] Engagement forms the conditions for user participation, and some of these conditions are automated (chapter 2). The more participation becomes automated, for example, through protocols that transform likes into advertisements visible on your friends' feeds, the more social media users are deprived of agency and turned into what Gilles Deleuze has called *dividuals* (chapter 1), Félix Guattari has described as *machinic subjectivities* (chapter 3), and John Cheney-Lippold has formulated as *algorithmic identities* (chapter 6). A beloved child has many names, as the Finnish proverb goes, and what is specifically beloved by social media platforms are the data profiles and consumer demographics generated and sold for marketing purposes (chapter 6).

It is in reaction to this engagement with the social media platform (chapter 1), commodification of personal user data, and the overall monetization of users that disconnection often emerges as a possibility or an act of resistance (chapters 2, 3, 5, and 6). Disconnection is something users can do (chapters 5 and 6), but disconnections can also take the form of media art (chapter 3) or be a service to which users subscribe (chapter 6). Disconnections are anticipated by the platforms and responded to at the level of interfaces (chapter 2) and future designs (chapter 1). After the process of memorializing Facebook users, even death no longer separates us from the platform (chapters 4 and 5), and the questions of user agency (chapter 5) and the possibility to disconnect (chapter 6) become central to our understandings of the power social media platforms hold and exercise.

While disconnecting from and with social media is problematized in this book in multiple ways, at the heart of the argument is the idea that disconnections carry a qualitative difference and challenge our current connections both in practice and in theory. Disconnections are considered, following Foucault, as breaks, ruptures, and interruptions that shape, transform, and mutate the formation of our current culture.[103] They are forces that belong to this culture as much as its dominant discursive formations and modes of power. Along with Foucault, I am building here on the foundations of the philosophy of becoming and difference presented by Deleuze, where things find their form through different assemblages and agents and difference is a productive force that makes virtuals actualize.[104] Deleuze argues that the problem with difference is that in the history of philosophy, it is too often understood through concepts of identity, opposition, analogy, and resemblance. For Deleuze, putting things into binary opposites means comparing them to each other. This difference as a product of comparison is measured according to sameness between these objects.

Difference in itself is not a secondary characteristic but needs to be considered as what it is. Difference in itself is not grounded in anything else (sameness, identity, analogy, etc.). Instead, as Cliff Stagoll argues, "difference is *internal* to a thing or event, implicit in its being that particular."[105] Disconnection, understood as difference, has the potential to be "difference in itself," freed from the metaphysically primary of connection.[106]

Building on this metaphysics of difference does not mean that disconnecting is elevated above connections but rather that it enables us to look at the limits of connectivity from within. Light ends his book on disconnection with the suggestion that the concept may force us to revisit the epistemological and ontological understandings of social media sites.[107] If talking about connective media instead of social media, as Van Dijck proposes, would move us from the framework of participation to questions of platform architecture and making things meaningful, what would the ontologies and epistemologies be if we were to start from disconnections instead? In lieu of an answer, the following chapters will map the features and characteristics of a culture of disconnectivity, which is out there and in here in our daily social media connections. The culture of disconnectivity is accompanied by social media and emerges together with it. Connectivity and disconnectivity are like the two horses in Plato's *Phaedrus* pulling the user in different directions.

In the following passages, I will show that *engage* and *participate* are the key order words of connectivity but also mechanisms of control that modulate and condition the user for the needs of the platform and social media business models in particular ways. Rather than beginning from the human perspective, these concepts force us to think about agency in the context of the platform. Different modes of agency are intrinsically tied with social media platforms' sociotechnical features and automation of not only the structures or systems under which we operate but also our behaviors, moods, and interactions. But these functions and connections also bring with them their disconnections. Here one is reminded of Paul Virilio's notion that accidents are always invented together with our technical objects: "oceangoing vessels invented the shipwreck, trains the rail catastrophe."[108] Similarly, disconnections are invented together with connections. These disconnections should not be reduced disengagements or nonparticipation, modes of withdrawal from the social, but be seen as processes that shape the social in social media in different ways. Disconnections contest our social media engagements. Disconnections emerge and evolve together with connections. If connectivity is a process of unity, disconnectivity is partial, dissonant, and even violent in its modes that interfere with that which is being unified. The appearances of disconnections may be scattered and brief but substantial in their effects; if the goal of social media platforms is to capture everything within and build a connected world, disconnections have the capability to "place thought in an immediate relation with the outside, with the forces of the outside."[109] Disconnections are tools to think about the outside; they destroy the all-too perfect and totalizing images of the world connected, showing that there are cracks everywhere through which the outside will get in. To open these cracks more, to bring the outside in, and to express the constant attempts by social media companies to protect against the outside, another set of order words is examined: *deactivate, die, log out,* and *disconnect.*

Engage

"Half of the world's estimated online population now check in to the social networking giant Facebook at least once a month," the news declares.[1] But Facebook's position as the biggest social media platform is still not secure. For years now, the press has been declaring the death of Facebook by pointing out that it is no longer a popular social media platform among teens and young people and sometimes drawing attention to campaigns like Quit Facebook Day or individual projects of digital detox. While Facebook is still going strong and its user base is growing, these discussions point to the fragility of its business. By looking at some previous social media sites, such as Friendster and MySpace, we see that threats can actualize suddenly and that mass exodus of users can bring the sites down. Friendster and MySpace are both examples of social media sites that had gathered a massive user base. Friendster in 2002 was one of the first sites to attract more than 1 million users, and in 2008, it had a base of more than 110 million registered users. Yet, its success did not last, and already by 2009, the satirical news site *The Onion* made a story of its decline where an "internet archeologist" claimed to have discovered the "ruins" of the Friendster "civilization." MySpace suffered a similar fate. In 2004, at the peak of its boom, MySpace even tried to acquire Facebook, but the price tag of $75 million scared MySpace off.[2] Eventually, as Facebook kept growing its active user base, both MySpace and Friendster faded. Robert W. Gehl has aptly argued that where MySpace failed at building "an architecture of abstraction in which users' affect and content were easily reduced to marketer friendly data sets," Facebook succeeded.[3]

Although it was Facebook that allegedly finished off MySpace and Friendster, it is easy to see that what happened to these social networking sites is haunting the future of Facebook's success:

> A number of other social networking companies that achieved early popularity have since seen their active user bases or levels of engagement decline, in some cases precipitously. There is no guarantee that we will not experience a similar erosion of our active user base or engagement levels.[4]

For Facebook, the potential of mass disconnection is present as a problem of management and control. At the heart of this challenge is the problem of how to manage the dynamics between the individual user and masses of users, that is, between individuals and populations. This problem, of course, is not solely Facebook's. In fact, it is a problem familiar to all entities that deal with masses of people, such as the nation-state, as articulated by Michel Foucault in his book *Security, Territory, and Population.*[5]

Tiziana Terranova has argued that Foucault gives us two ways to approach social media connectivity: one focusing on its *disciplinary mechanisms,* the other on *dispositifs of security.*[6] Both relate to how Foucault describes changes in the mechanisms of control when populations become problematic for nation-states. Disciplinary control is centripetal and works by confining people to certain locations. Foucault's own example, of course, is Jeremy Bentham's Panopticon—a prison designed in the late eighteenth century.[7] The Panopticon consists of a circular structure of cells with a watchtower in the middle. This design allows a watchman to observe all inmates of the institution without them being able to tell whether they are being watched at any time. What the Panopticon for Foucault illustrates is a transition from surveillance to self-regulation. The possibility of being constantly watched produces subjects who adjust their behavior under the assumption that they indeed are constantly watched. As Bucher notes, for Foucault, power here has a technical form; it is organized by a contingent architectural apparatus of the prison.[8] This apparatus breaks the crowd and produces a collection of separate individualities not only subjected to monitoring but also constantly monitoring themselves.[9] With security, the goal is not to confine people or things to a certain location that can be monitored. In fact, the target of security is not individuals but crowds and masses, populations. The strategies of confinement, such as building walled cities and fixing people to particular locations, become impossible when populations begin to grow rapidly. As cities become overcrowded, it becomes essential to be able to mobilize these masses and control their flow. Controlling populations becomes an issue of "making possible, guaranteeing, and ensuring circulation" of people.[10] Paraphrasing Foucault, Terranova remarks that the "problem of security is the problem of circulation which will be solved by trying to 'plan a milieu in terms of events or series of events or possible elements, of series that will have to be regulated within a multivalent and transformable framework.'"[11] According to Foucault, the milieu is both "a medium of an action and the element in which it circulates," and the "apparatuses of security work, fabricate, organize, and plan a milieu even before the notion was formed and isolated. The milieu, then, will be that in which circulation is carried out."[12] The milieu of security extends not only to individuals but to all things and relations that define people and their movements, from wealth and resources to territories, customs, and bonds and, finally, to diseases, accidents, and threats.[13]

Terranova maintains that from the Foucauldian perspective, social media discussions have been focusing on the notion of the panopticon and how social media users operate in a system of surveillance, but Foucault's notion of security also gives us a view of how social media systems try to stabilize their position by "maximizing circulation, minimizing error or loss and ensuring an overall expansive stability, an indefinite homeostasis able to withstand and re-absorb the uncertain and aleatory event of social Subjectivation."[14] This logic, which Terranova calls in the context of social media "securing the social," becomes emphasized when Facebook needs to manage the risk of disconnection.[15] What follows is a social media strategy that expands social media connections everywhere and intensifies them to maximize circulation of content, data, and users. Following Foucault, this logic takes place in the conjunction of a "series of events produced by individuals, populations, and groups, and quasi natural events which occur around them."[16]

Maximizing circulation and ensuring expansive stability are questions of risk management. To be clear, these risks do not only loom in the background. Quite on the contrary, risks demand solutions. These solutions are preemptive by nature. Solutions try to condition the present so that the risks never actualize. Ulises A. Mejias writes that we need to analyze the means social media networks use to protect themselves against risks.[17] Specifically, he notes that it is not uncommon for social media platforms and networks to use "disasters and failures to redraw [their] boundaries and strengthen [their] borders against anything that might threaten [their] logic."[18] This notion is affirmed in the "Risk Factors" section of Facebook's *2015 Annual Report,* which articulates the ways in which Facebook tries to manage and control its user base against the threat mass disconnection poses:

> We anticipate that our active user growth rate will continue to
> decline over time as the size of our active user base increases, and
> as we achieve higher market penetration rates. . . . If our active
> user growth rate continues to slow, we will become increasingly
> dependent on our ability to maintain or increase levels of user
> engagement and monetization in order to drive revenue growth.[19]

Facebook's financial documents give the control mechanism Facebook implements a particular name: *user engagement.* In the following passages, I conceptually formulate what is meant by user engagement, and I trace how maintaining and monetizing user engagement grounds Facebook's operational logic and is correlated with the company's future product developments. This logic and its manifestations need to be analyzed from the perspective of disconnection and the potential of mass exodus. User engagement is a relation threatened by disconnection, and simultaneously, disconnection becomes the basis for establishing stronger user engagement.[20]

User Engagement

User engagement is at the heart of Facebook's business: "If we fail to retain existing users or add new users, or if our users decrease their level of engagement with our products, our revenue, financial results, and business may be significantly harmed."[21] Reading Facebook's financial documents reveals that user engagement is the main concept the company uses to describe both user-to-user and user-to-platform relations that happen on Facebook, but this concept is hardly defined either by businesses or social media researchers. One particular exception is given in *Spreadable Media* by Henry Jenkins, Sam Ford, and Joshua Green, in which they describe user engagement through a comparison between engagement-based business models and appointment-based models of the U.S. television industry.[22] The main difference according to Jenkins et al. is that the appointment-based models are centralized, whereas the engagement-based models are decentralized. In the former, content is created and distributed primarily through one channel at one particular time, and in the latter, the content is distributed through multiple means, and viewers are actively involved with the content as redistributors and recommenders. According to Jenkins and coauthors, the engagement-based business models try "to capture and capitalize on the public's desire to participate."[23]

Participation for Jenkins et al. supersedes things like the platform as modes of organizing the social; the social for them is always first human sociality, human participation, and human communication, whether mediated by a certain platform or not.[24] From a nonhuman perspective, however, user engagement cannot be framed solely through user participation. The problem here, to put it bluntly, is seeing engagement as a unidirectional, human-to-human relation, and platforms are secondary to human actions. Arguably, user engagement is a more complex relation. It is a relation not only of user to user but of user to platform. User engagement, then, is a relation that does not privilege users or platforms. It is a threshold between the two.[25]

I do agree with Jenkins, Ford, and Green that the language and metaphors we use when we speak of social media not only describe the patterns we see taking place but also shape our assumptions about and actions in response to those patterns.[26] From this perspective, it is very interesting and telling that the phrase "user participation" so dominant to our understanding of social media *never* appears in Facebook's S-1 filing report, which illustrates its business for potential investors.[27] For me, this underlines the fact that business strategies that exploit the voluntary involvement of users are only one part of engagement-based business models. Another side of these models is the mechanisms that capture social and all other relations happening on the platform, turn them into marketable data. This is not a paranoid proposition but a logic that is transparently visible if one looks at how Facebook can be used for advertising.

For example, Facebook's help page for businesses, titled "How to

Target Facebook Ads," gives us an example of how the information you provide for the platform is constantly used to decide what ads you will see next.[28] According to the site, "one of the biggest advantages to advertising on Facebook is your ability to target specific groups of highly engaged people. In fact, compared to the average online reach of 38% for narrowly targeted campaigns, Facebook is 89% accurate."[29] Advertisers are given the opportunity to target engaged Facebook users based on "location," "demographics," "interests," and "behaviors." If the advertiser chooses to target by location, Facebook uses both the location information users give the platform and the locations of users' IP addresses to determine where the users are. If the advertiser chooses to target users based on demographics, Facebook uses the information about age, gender, education, and workplace that users have given the platform about themselves. Similarly, information about "interests" is mined from users' Facebook Timelines. It can consist, for example, of hobbies the users have listed but may also derive from Facebook Pages the users have liked. The click of the like button here increases the list of interests. "Behaviors" is perhaps the most interesting category, because it explicitly shows how our engagements with Facebook are engagements that cannot be reduced to the mere use of the platform. According to Facebook, "behaviors are activities that people do on or off Facebook that inform on which device they're using, purchase behaviors or intents, travel preferences and more. Behaviors are constructed from both someone's activity on Facebook and offline activity provided by data from Facebook's trusted third-party partners."[30]

The tips provided on the "How to Target Facebook Ads" web page should not be read only as instrumental directions for how to use Facebook for marketing; rather, they explicate how the platform enables circulation between engaged users and the material they share both voluntarily and involuntarily. In particular, the important role of enabling circulation is manifested in Facebook's principle called *frictionless sharing,* which was introduced in September 2011 at Facebook's annual F8 developer conference.[31] Frictionless sharing was dubbed as Facebook's "new way to express who you are," and it was accompanied with the Timeline as a major interface update and with the Open Graph protocol as a system to handle the "distribution of content" and to let "website owners trace the paths their content takes, thereby organizing the relation between content and users."[32]

Robert Payne points out that from Facebook's perspective, all user activities can be defined as sharing.[33] Frictionless sharing, according to Payne, is a construction of mediated liveness, where everything a user does is automatically at least potentially shared with other users in that network in real time.[34] Payne analyzes how frictionless sharing has been received and analyzed by the tech blogs, noting how they raise the concern of its social and cultural effects. According to Payne, tech bloggers were maintaining the ethos of Henry Jenkins, "who insists that circulation of media objects occurs in function of their adaptable meaningfulness to individual media consumers. It is not the interface but the *users* who collectively and actively 'spread' that object."[35] For Payne, one important example comes from a CNET blogger, Molly Wood, who claims that

> sharing and recommendation shouldn't be passive. It should be conscious, thoughtful, and amusing—we are tickled by a story, picture, or video and we choose to share it, and if a startling number of Internet users also find that thing amusing, we, together, consciously create a tidal wave of meme that elevates that piece of media to viral status. We choose these gems from the noise. Open Graph will fill our feeds with noise, burying the gems.[36]

According to Payne, these discourses reflect the fear that participation on social media is becoming automated and that content, whatever that might be, spreads like a virus without human choice or the possibility to manage what one is sharing online.[37]

Terranova notes that what is novel with digital social networks is the way they capture social relations within their marketing and monetizing mechanisms.[38] This is exemplified by the instructions of "How to Target Facebook Ads." Facebook expands to different fields of human life through our multiple online engagements, where social relations are one, and then these relations are intensified as functions or involvements with the platform through frictionless sharing. Subsequently, these engagements become monetized.

What is needed is a reevaluation of the user engagement–based business models by Jenkins et al. in the context of Facebook's engagement policy. Instead of contextualizing engagement as distributed and user-centric, here we encounter an alternative understanding of engagement-based business models that cannot be reduced to user participation. In this model, as Carolin Gerlitz and Anne Helmond argue, Facebook is

> not only a social web, but also a recentralised, data-intensive
> infrastructure. . . . In this Like economy, the social is of particular
> economic value, as user interactions are instantly transformed into
> comparable forms of data and presented to other users in a way
> that generates more traffic and engagement.[39]

Here decentralized users are recentralized by the data-intensive infra-structure of the platform, and the "platform advances an alternative form of connectivity which is operating in the back end and which facilitates participation in Facebook's Like economy by default."[40] In this model of engagement-based businesses, the users are still content producers, but they operate under the conditions established and maintained by the centralized platform. Frictionless sharing intensifies all engagements with the platform, and users are forced to partici-pate in the processes of data mining and monetization of those data, whether or not they actively decide to do so.

Dividuals

If user engagement is the proto-relation according to which Facebook's business models operate, and if it is in fact different from user partici-pation, it becomes necessary to revisit the concept of engagement. Let me begin with the etymology of the concept. The noun *engagement* is derived from the verb *engage*. According to the *Oxford Living Dic-tionaries*, the origin of the word engage is

> Late Middle English (formerly also as ingage): from French
> engager, ultimately from the base of gage. The word originally
> meant "to pawn or pledge something," later "pledge oneself (to do
> something)," hence "enter into a contract" (mid 16th century),
> "involve oneself in an activity," "enter into combat" (mid 17th
> century), giving rise to the notion "involve someone or something
> else."[41]

Furthermore, the same dictionary notes that the noun *gage* is "a valued object deposited as a guarantee of good faith" and that the verb denotes an "offer (an object or one's life) as a guarantee of good faith."[42] What I want to highlight here is that engagement as derived from the words *gage* and *engage* implies a relation that is in itself economic. Engagement is a contract or a pledge, even a pawn or mortgage that secures and guarantees. Engagement means becoming involved with something, but importantly, it does not define an activity (such as participation); it merely ensures that there will be an activity. Engagement creates a field of intensity.

This idea of field of intensity is in debt to Brian Massumi's discussion of affect as intensity and his notion that "intensity is embodied in purely autonomic reactions most directly manifested in the skin—at the surface of the body, at its interface with things."[43] When Massumi directs the attention to body as the main unit of experiencing intensities, he is not claiming that intensities happen only in the haptic register but rather that the intensities operate beyond meaning, language, or the mind. As he notes,

> intensity is . . . a nonconscious, never-to-be-conscious autonomic
> remainder. It is outside expectation and adaptation, as disconnected
> from meaningful sequencing, from narration, as it is from vital
> function. It is narratively de-localized, spreading over the general-
> ized body surface, like a lateral backwash from the function-
> meaning interloops traveling the vertical path between head and
> heart.[44]

What the field of intensity does is activate us as Facebook users. When engaged with the platform, our bodies become enabled by its processes and affordances "but also in terms of what may be mobilized or released when they come into odd conjunction with another scale, dimension of relationality, or drive."[45] In other words, intensities are not only experienced by bodies passing from one state to another but the field of intensities produces the event of passing when users are engaged with the platform.

Facebook brings together two billion users, and while these users are unique, that is, "they carry a different set of tendencies and capacities,"[46] they are still indexed to the same shocks and cues when they log in to their Facebook accounts. The relations users have on Facebook are intensified not only in the sense that they are affective but also in the sense that they are technologically mediated and structured by the process of the platform. In the simplest sense, this means that we chat through Messenger, update our daily happenings through the News Feed, and express our relations with the Like button. All these Facebook features set a particular field of intensity with the capability to attune our bodies. As a result of this process of attunement, we become part of a collective that clicks the Like button or communicates through Messenger or constantly monitors their News Feeds.

A corollary for my proposition to rethink what we mean by engagement is that we also need a specific understanding of what is meant by the user. One way to think about the user in this context comes from Gilles Deleuze's "Postscript on the Societies of Control," where he builds on Foucault's notion of security as a particular mechanism of control in societies that are run and governed with code and computational technologies.[47] Deleuze argues that in societies of control, we are no longer dealing with a "mass/individual pair"; rather, "individuals have become '*dividuals*,' and masses, samples, data, markets, or '*banks*.'"[48] For Deleuze, dividuals are numerical bodies of code that exist both online and offline, endlessly being split by the relations between these two regimes.

The examples of Facebook advertising that puts users in categories based on their behaviors or demographics show the Deleuzian dividual in action. According to Kevin Haggerty and Richard Ericson, these systems turn individuals into "data doubles," which are "used to create consumer profiles, refine service delivery and target specific markets."[49] For example, if you are marketing on Facebook, you can use a feature called Lookalike Audience.[50] First, you upload a list of at least one hundred existing customers on Facebook. Then you can use that group as reference data for Lookalike Audience, which finds and matches your customer list with people with similar interests on Facebook. Lookalike Audience disassembles users by extracting data from their interactions and then reassembles them from different flows of data. What emerges from this reassembling are data doubles that "ostensibly refer back to particular individuals," but rather than being "accurate or inaccurate portrayals of real individuals, they are a form of pragmatics: differentiated according to how useful they are in allowing institutions to make discriminations among populations."[51]

However, I want to show here that the dividual is not only a data double between online and offline but is a more generative state produced by our engagements with Facebook. In fact, the field of intensity produced by engagement presupposes that we are dividuals in the first place. Here I am following Massumi, for whom the dividual is not a data double but rather a more fundamental division in the fabric of the existence of each individual.[52] For Massumi, the dividual addresses how each individual is already split between the rational and the affective. Massumi's example of the dividual is the individual subject of interest as the fundamental unit of capitalist society. The individual subject of interest is what Gabriel Tarde describes as *homo economicus,* an individual "who would exclusively and methodically pursue his egoistical interest—having abstracted from every feeling, faith or partisanship."[53] According to Tarde, when economists describe the individual, they make two misleading reductions. First, they remove the heart of the human from the equation; that is, they assume that the individual subject of interest is purely rational and does not follow her feelings or moods. Second, they detach the individual from his associations with groups, homelands, corporations, and so on. These two reductions compose the affective side of the individual. That is to say, for the individual, rational decision-making is always influenced by affective associations of moods and groups. Massumi calls this level the infra-individual.[54] He notes that it is a level that expresses itself especially when decision-making deals with the uncertainty of the future.[55] In decisions that relate to the unknown, the individual is left to rely on her moods and the tendencies of the others.[56]

Arguably, the individual subject of interest has also been the subject of our many current notions of social media as participatory culture. A social media user who pursues their interests when participating and exploiting the wealth of the networks is the *homo economicus* per se. But simultaneously, when we participate in these processes, our engagements always split us between the rational user who participates and the affected/affective user who becomes engaged with the field of intensity often irrationally and without our conscious control. Whereas the former is tuned at the level of individuals and their interactions, the latter, as Tony Sampson points out, happens at the infra-level, "below cognitive awareness of social associations."[57]

When Massumi says that the individual is dividual, he means that we are always being split between the rational and the affective in a sense that does not form binary relations. Rather, microlevel and infra-level resonate with each other in oscillatory processes that cannot be separated into different occurrences. As Tarde states,

> never, in any period of history, have a producer and a consumer, a seller and a buyer been in each other's presence without having first been united to one another by some entirely sentimental relation being neighbours, sharing citizenship or religious communion, enjoying a community of civilisation and, second, without having been, respectively, escorted by an invisible cortege of associates, friends, and coreligionists whose thought has weighed on them in the discussion of prices or wages, and has finally won out, most often to the detriment of their strictly individual interest.[58]

Although the period Tarde discusses is the turn of the 1900s, the description seems to be even more accurate in our current moment of online connectivity, where connections are mediated by social media platforms and opinions formed not only by peers of users but also by algorithmic marketing mechanisms.

The sentimental relations to others here are not so much individual feelings experienced as precognitive attachments affecting individual interests and rational decision-making. As Massumi phrased it, "rational decision is unconditionally, irreducibly, nontransferably referred to an infra-individual zone of in-distinction with affect."[59] What the understanding of the individual as dividual for Massumi provides is a way to think about how collective and transformative action can take place outside self-interest. For me, this is also a way to understand user engagement with social media. Thinking about users as dividuals and user engagement as a field of intensity moves us from thinking what user engagement is to what *user engagement does*. The population control of the one billion means pushing and pulling us toward novel engagements. These engagements alter our interactions with each other and with the platform.

Platform

The dividual is an important concept because it brings us to the difference between how online communities and online populations are conceived. Online communities are seen as an aggregation of individuals who interact around a shared interest, and this interaction is mediated by a particular online platform. Online populations, I would argue, do not share an interest, for how could two billion share anything that is not abstracted to the point that it becomes redundant, such as humanity or culture? Rather, an online platform turns masses into populations by producing their interests and by conditioning their interactions. To make this difference is not to say that these two elements are separate but rather to show, following Massumi, that "beneath the microeconomic level of the individual there is an infra-economic level" that affects users and their behaviors.[60]

This, for me, is the starting point for platform politics. Social platforms from early on were designed to exploit and condition their users. For example, Tim O'Reilly (2005) notes that

> Web 2.0 is the network as platform, spanning all connected
> devices; Web 2.0 applications are those that make the most of the
> intrinsic advantages of that platform: delivering software as a
> continually-updated service that gets better the more people use it,
> consuming and remixing data from multiple sources, including
> individual users, while providing their own data and services in a
> form that allows remixing by others, creating network effects
> through an "architecture of participation," and going beyond the
> page metaphor of Web 1.0 to deliver rich user experiences.[61]

"Platform," as argued by Anne Helmond, among others, "has become the dominant concept for social media companies for positioning themselves in the market and addressing users."[62] On June 1, 2007, Facebook gave us a technical explanation for what it means by a platform: Facebook Platform is designed to enable third-party developers to design and "integrate their applications into Facebook—into the social graph—the same way that our [Facebook's] applications like Photos and Notes are integrated."[63] The platform is designed to act like a centrifugal force expanding everywhere and integrating everything within the site. In July 2008, in a press release titled "Facebook Expands Power of Platform across the Web and around the World," the company illustrates the ever expanding power of the platform:

> "We opened Facebook Platform with a belief that community
> innovation can give people the tools, and the power, to share and
> communicate in ways that Facebook can't build on its own. We're
> humbled by what our developer community has accomplished,"

said Mark Zuckerberg, founder and CEO of Facebook. "We're confident that the changes we're presenting today help developers build more meaningful social applications that enable users to share more information."[64]

Although, for Facebook, *platform* is a technical concept, the field of media theory has increasingly adopted this concept to outline how social media companies use software, as Helmond describes, "in shaping participation and sociality."[65] Platforms establish the conditions for anything from communication to sharing and interaction to take place; they are conduits of governance at the levels of hardware, software, and users, as Ganaele Langlois puts it.[66]

Again we can see this trend emerging in the first discussions of social media platforms. In 2006, O'Reilly argued that "Web 2.0 is the business revolution in the computer industry caused by the move to the internet as platform, and an attempt to understand the rules for success on that new platform. Chief among those rules is this: Build applications that harness network effects to get better the more people use them." While this rule has dominated our understanding of social media, the second rule O'Reilly makes has for me equal importance from the perspective of platform politics: "Don't treat software as an artifact, but as a process of engagement with your users."[67] With these two rules, O'Reilly draws two boundaries according to which social media sites currently try to manage the risk of losing their user populations. The problem is how to tie the dividual more deeply within Facebook's mechanisms of value production, and the solution comes in the form of the platform. The platform needs to be designed not only for individual users but also for masses of users. And simultaneously, the platform needs to address each individual user independently, forming relationships of engagement and building fields of intensity.

Facebook's annual reports quite explicitly state that when its user base is under threat, these two rules apply. For example, in 2015, Facebook says that its business performance will become increasingly dependent on its ability to increase levels of user engagement and monetization.[68] To restate, when Facebook is in a situation where its user base no longer grows endlessly, its business is increasingly dependent on two things: (1) its ability to "increase levels of user engagement" and (2) "monetization" of existing relations of engagement.[69] In other words, to survive, Facebook needs to expand and intensify: *expand the possibilities* of user engagement and *intensify the existing relations of user engagement,* and the platform is the medium between these two dimensions.

Facebook's financial documents illustrate that the ability to control its user population both defines the company's limits and ensures its survival. Here the axioms of expansion and intensification correlate with Foucault's centrifugal and centripetal understandings of security. On one hand, user engagement is moving or tending to move away from a center, as in expanding to everywhere and everything, and on the other hand, it is moving or tending to move toward a center that is intensifying all the relations and making them Facebook compatible. Facebook's economic rationality is based on circulation. To paraphrase Foucault, whether it is people, stocks, or grain, this rationality tries to make possible, guarantee, and ensure "circulations: the circulation of people, merchandise, and air, etcetera."[70] Instead of confining, privatizing, and enclosing in the manner of disciplinary control, security expands and integrates: "new elements are constantly being integrated: production, psychology, behavior, the ways of doing things of producers, buyers, consumers, importers, and exporters, and the world market"—security "lets things happen," as Foucault puts it.[71]

In the remaining passages, user engagement is traced through this particular double logic or double movement between expansion and intensification, platform and frictionless sharing. This double logic is attached to Facebook's attempts to redraw and strengthen its borders against the looming threat of disconnection. In particular, we see it actualizing in Facebook's future product developments, in which the relationship of user engagement has a primary role: "We prioritize product development investments that we believe will create engaging interactions between our users, developers and marketers," Facebook states in its *2015 Annual Report.*[72]

Movement 1: Money

In the "Risk Factors" section of its *2015 Annual Report,* Facebook states, "Any decrease in user retention, growth, or engagement could render our products less attractive to users, marketers, and developers, which is likely to have a material and adverse impact on our revenue, business, financial condition, and results of operations."[73] By looking at Facebook's current and future product developments, I will theorize how Facebook responds to the risk of disconnection and how these responses produce a relation that I have been formulating as user engagement. Let me begin with monetization and two Facebook features, one in beta-test mode and another available for everyone: the Buy button and Payments in Messenger features.

The Buy button is Facebook's concrete way to monetize the affective streams that invite us to click and simultaneously to accumulate concrete information about what users of certain demographic cluster are purchasing. The test phase for the Buy button began in July 2014. According to Facebook, "we're beginning to test a new feature to help businesses drive sales through Facebook in News Feed and on Pages."[74] This is basically how it goes: an advertiser buys a sponsored story from Facebook and inserts a Buy button into that post, and when the user sees the post, he can click the Buy button to make the purchase. With the Buy button, "people on desktop or mobile can click the 'Buy' call-to-action button on ads and Page posts to purchase a product directly from a business, without leaving Facebook." The Buy button functions entirely within Facebook throughout the whole purchase process. With the Buy button, Facebook is no longer an access point or advertising platform for online retailers. Instead, online shopping is subsumed within the platform; the platform is turned into a marketplace. Here the Buy button expands the platform toward online retailing but also and simultaneously monetizes existing user relations by providing a way to respond to advertising without leaving the site.[75]

The second new button appears on Facebook Messenger. While using Facebook Messenger to chat with other users, you may have noticed that in the right-hand corner is a dollar icon. Clicking the icon, you can now send money to the other user via Facebook Messenger. This new feature, named Payments in Messenger, is Facebook's recent way to ensure that capital circulates on the platform. Indeed, Payments in Messenger is a direct approach to building economic transactions between users on Facebook. According to Facebook's Help Center:

> you can send or receive money in Messenger (ex: send your friend $10 for lunch or receive $500 from your roommate for rent) after you add a debit card issued by a US bank to your account and

install the latest version of Messenger. Once you add a debit card, you can create a PIN to provide extra security the next time you send money.[76]

Interestingly, Facebook does not charge users for making economic transactions on the platform. Messenger is not a feature that produces direct monetary value. Quite paradoxically, its enabling of the circulation of money needs to be interpreted through other possible measurements of value. Here thinking about Payments in Messenger through Georg Simmel's *Philosophy of Money* would prove useful in its elaboration of economic and noneconomic values of money.[77] Trust is Simmel's prime example of a noneconomic value. Exchanges of money are dependent on trust on a number of levels. Exchanges of money involve trust among people who do the transactions, but even more importantly, they involve trust in the conditions that control these transactions. For Simmel, this leads to the development of centralized control in the form of the modern state and its juridical system.

In the case of Facebook, a similar movement is visible. By expanding the platform toward monetary transactions, Facebook intensifies the relations we have on the platform. Our user engagement becomes a contract between the platform and other users of the platform, in which each user at least potentially agrees to do, make, buy, or sell a good or service or grants a right or undertakes an obligation to do so.

Our engagements become glazed with a new layer of trust needed for monetary transactions. Both the Buy button and Payments in Messenger establish and re-valuate the social relationships users have both with each other and on the platform. When money and exchanges of money enter the picture, questions of trust and control emerge. Through our engagements with the site, the pawn we give is our actual identity. To rephrase, Buy button and Payments in Messenger do not only enable monetary transactions; they also affirm and emphasize user identities. Debit cards, at least in the United States, are not only used as a method of payment but can also work as a secondary proof of identity. When you operate with state officials, you can use the card to prove who you are. Payment cards move the user toward an "engagement with a form of social and economic life that is saturated with multiple, variably enacted and enacting, socio-material devices," as Joe Deville notes.[78]

When the user submits her method for payment on Facebook, she will at the same time also provide proof of her identity. Proving one's identity with a payment card generates a relationship of trust between the networks of individuals on Facebook and with the platform. Here trust, or the feeling of trust, affectively attunes the user. If the platform is safe for monetary transactions, it is safe, private, and trustworthy enough for anything else. In this context, expansion and intensification are not only material but also psychological and mental issues. Facebook's expansion toward financial services is also a question of intensification of the relations of trust we have with the platform and with other users on the platform.

Payments in Messenger and the Buy button are examples of the monetization of social media relations. They are also concrete examples of how social media are "engineering our connectivity"[79] by constantly integrating new things, functions, and services into their system. What can be integrated also dictates how social relations, cultural practices, and public and private services can be rethought and repurposed. For example, according to the *Financial Times,*

> the social network is only weeks away from obtaining regulatory approval in Ireland for a service that would allow its users to store money on Facebook and use it to pay and exchange money with others, according to several people involved in the process. The authorisation from Ireland's central bank to become an "e-money" institution would allow Facebook to issue units of stored monetary value that represent a claim against the company. This e-money would be valid throughout Europe via a process known as "passporting."[80]

This is not the only case where Facebook's power to change the banking industry has been noted in the press. *Wired* reports that national regulations, for example, in the European Union, are changing toward "open banking" so that nonbanks such as Facebook can be used to access one's bank account to make payments.[81] Some of the banks are already testing banking with Facebook; the ATB bank, for example, is the "first full-service financial institution in North America to successfully facilitate payments using chatbot technology on Facebook Messenger."[82] Facebook can be seen not only changing the banking industry but also challenging it in the future. "Roughly one in three banking and insurance customers globally would consider switching their accounts to Google (GOOGL.O), Amazon (AMZN.O) or Facebook (FB.O) if the Silicon Valley giants offered financial services," Reuters tells us, referring to a survey conducted by Accenture.[83] Based on these examples, using a payment card for purchases or transferring money via the platform may be only a small part of the financial services Facebook could deliver in the future. The *Financial Times* news story implies with a voice of "a person familiar with the company's strategy" that the question we should be asking is not how but where; "Facebook wants to become a utility in the developing world, and remittances are a gateway drug to financial inclusion."[84]

Movement 2: Internet.org

The emerging markets, the developing world, the not-yet-connected three billion potential users, are, according to Zuckerberg's letter for prospective Facebook investors, the company's key strategic area:

> There is a huge need and a huge opportunity to get everyone in the world connected, to give everyone a voice and to help transform society for the future. The scale of the technology and infrastructure that must be built is unprecedented, and we believe this is the most important problem we can focus on.[85]

Facebook has taken an active role in supporting and building global connectivity through an initiative it calls Internet.org. According to Facebook, "the goal of Internet.org is to make internet access available to the two-thirds of the world who are not yet connected, and to bring the same opportunities to everyone that the connected third of the world has today."[86] Zuckerberg notes that "when communities are connected, we can lift them out of poverty."[87] Interestingly, the discourses of Internet.org do not address Facebook and its practical solutions to ending poverty but rather the attention is directed toward a more general level of connective technologies and infrastructures. The implication here is that connections in themselves transform societies and that the power structures behind who owns, builds, and controls these connections are less significant.[88]

On March 28, 2014, Internet.org published Zuckerberg's thoughts on how this connectivity could be established in a memo titled "Connecting the World from the Sky."[89] In this document, Zuckerberg notes that Facebook wants to get rid of some of the "physical barriers to connectivity" and that it is "investing in building technologies to deliver new types of connectivity on the ground, in the air and in space."[90] For example, Facebook's recently established Connectivity Lab is tackling the issues of expansion of the internet infrastructure in a very literal sense. Says Zuckerberg, "In our effort to connect the whole world . . . , we've been working on ways to beam internet to people from the sky. Today, we're sharing some details of the work Facebook's Connectivity Lab is doing to build drones, satellites and lasers to deliver the internet to everyone."[91] Facebook's solar-powered drones would, for example, operate within the altitudes of sixty thousand to ninety thousand feet.[92] The "Connecting the World from the Sky" memo further explains these plans. The drones would fly outside of regulated airspace, they could provide internet connectivity to a "city-sized area of territory," and they could stay there for months or years. Facebook's Low Earth Orbit satellites could be deployed from 160 to 2,000 kilometers from earth and cover small-population-density areas. One problem with these satellites would be that they do not rotate in sync with the Earth, and hence a constellation of these satellites would be needed to establish continuous connectivity. Another solution for this problem could be the Geosynchronous Orbit satellites, which would be located "35,786 kilometers above sea level" and be pointed to one location indefinitely.[93]

On October 5, 2015, Facebook notified that at least one version of the satellites is becoming reality. In a Facebook status update, Zuckerberg told his friends and followers:

> I'm excited to announce our first project to deliver internet from
> space. As part of our Internet.org efforts to connect the world,
> we're partnering with Eutelsat to launch a satellite into orbit that
> will connect millions of people. . . . Connectivity changes lives and
> communities. We're going to keep working to connect the entire
> world—even if that means looking beyond our planet.[94]

Connecting the planet from the sky seems hardly a neutral project; instead, it can be interpreted as being a part of a new scientific-technological layering of planet Earth by media technologies, on one hand, and the commercialization of aerospace, on the other. Our current internet infrastructure is grounded on its surface;[95] for example, the internet connects different continents through a physical infrastructure of submarine cables owned and controlled mainly by private ventures.[96] Taking internet infrastructure off the ground into airspace, or rather into aerospace, can be seen as a geopolitical move on a global scale. The submarine cables going through nation-states have made the internet vulnerable to national conflicts[97] and also subjected it to different national rules and regulations. Because there are no international agreements on the vertical extent of sovereign airspace, the question of power becomes much more ambiguous, opening up room for different players and motivations.

With the Facebook drone and the satellite, Facebook is transforming the infrastructure that gives us access to the internet and engaging us with a system of its own. Another mode of engagement is the Free Basics Platform, which is part of Internet.org and designed to give free access only to a restricted number of sites on the internet.[98] In other words, the objective of Internet.org is to build a software platform that everyone uses but also to establish the infrastructural conditions through which any software platform can operate. Internet.org promises to bypass traditional internet service providers and allow free access to the selected internet sites, including Facebook, of course. This is also the reason why Internet.org has been widely criticized: it redirects our engagements and commercializes the infrastructure of the internet.[99] To be clear, these technologies are not only expansive technologies that will enable internet connectivity globally; they also capture the existing online connections, intensify them, and monetize them.

Conclusion

User engagement–based businesses are centralized by the platform. Through engagement, users involve themselves in an activity; they attach themselves into a field of intensity. User engagement is massive-scale affective contagion through the social media platform operating on the level of the infra-individual. Through user engagement, we are all individually and collectively connected to a field of intensity that moves, triggers, transmits, and transduces. User engagement secures Facebook's business first by constituting the conditions for user participation and second by dissolving the acts of participation into two concurrent streams. The first stream is the stream of data mined from everything we do on the platform and sites associated with the platform. The second stream is the stream of affective flows that intensify our interactions, move us, attune us toward different actions, operations, and modes of being. These streams are being successfully monetized with mechanisms such as targeted Facebook ads and frictionless sharing, which entices us to share more both voluntarily and involuntarily. These mechanisms make possible, guarantee, and ensure circulation. We are taken into circulation; we become part of Facebook as streams and flows of content.

When Facebook pushes and pulls us toward different engagements—the Buy button, Payments in Messenger, Internet.org—these engagements alter our interactions with one another and with the platform. These engagements are propositioned over a promise of immediacy of enjoyment and purpose.[100] But enjoyment and purpose are not individual feelings that come from our participation; rather, they are collective feelings produced by Facebook as a platform that, through expansions and intensifications, condition our experiences by affecting us individually and infra-individually.

To return to the point made at the beginning of this chapter, to prevent disconnection in the form of mass exodus from happening, Facebook uses tactics designed to govern populations rather than individuals. This is the reason why Facebook's financial documents hardly discuss participation and focus on engagement instead: participation is individual, whereas engagement is infra-individual. By expanding everywhere and intensifying our connections, Facebook tries to engage us as a collective. For it is engagement, not participation, that attunes us together toward a state where leaving Facebook becomes impossible both physically and mentally, individually and collectively. What also follows is the need to reconfigure how participation is understood in social media. This is the task of the next chapter, which focuses on Facebook's Timeline interface.

Participate

"Today, I am surrendering my Facebook account, because my participation on the site is simply too inconsistent with the values I espouse in my work," media theorist Douglas Rushkoff declares in 2013, in a manifesto published by CNN and titled "Why I'm Quitting Facebook."[1] In the manifesto, Rushkoff—who has been one of the most prominent voices resisting the dominance of social media platforms—explains his motivations behind his decision to refuse to use Facebook.

For Rushkoff, the enjoyment and purposefulness we feel when we participate with our social media connections are sustained by an illusion that we are in control of our social media lives. But platforms like Facebook, according to him, also do "things on our behalf when we're not even there. It [Facebook] actively misrepresents us to our friends, and worse misrepresents those who have befriended us to still others."[2] Rushkoff, in his criticism, is addressing a particular Facebook feature called Sponsored Stories, which was introduced in 2011 and dropped by the company in 2014. Sponsored Stories turned Facebook users and their clicks and likes into advertisements. Sponsored Stories were displayed on Facebook's News Feed stream alongside other status updates and things shared, and they consisted, for example, of the businesses or products one's friends had liked. According Rushkoff, "any of our updates might be converted into 'sponsored stories' by whatever business or brand we may have mentioned. That innocent mention of a cup of coffee at Starbucks, in the Facebook universe, quickly becomes an attributed endorsement of their brand."[3] In 2014, Sponsored Stories was removed, but a similar advertising mechanism subsists on the platform, where a user's "profile picture or name may be paired with an ad" to show their "activity on Facebook."[4]

Although for some users these advertisements may be useful in helping them choose different products based on their friends' preferences or likes, Sponsored Stories, the feature, was for Rushkoff the last straw and a sufficient reason to disconnect Facebook. Adjusting to new interfaces and changes in privacy settings has often been addressed as a particular concern for social media users.[5] For the research on disconnection, these are interesting moments, because, paraphrasing Anne Kaun and Christian Schwarzenegger, when particular social media features lead into disconnection, it also opens a way to navigate our networked society and its constitutive experiences from a different perspective.[6] What Rushkoff's commentary highlights is that users are valuable for Facebook, but their participation is not given. While the platform is constantly establishing new modes of participation, it also must be ready to give up the ones that are not successful or well received. Sponsored Stories is part of Facebook's experiments with modes of user participation that would be automated by the platform and operate beyond the users' control or choice while still carrying their names. For users like Rushkoff, Sponsored Stories revealed Facebook's true nature:

> Facebook has never been merely a social platform. Rather, it
> exploits our social interactions the way a Tupperware party does.
> Facebook does not exist to help us make friends, but to turn our
> network of connections, brand preferences and activities over
> time—our "social graphs"—into money for others.[7]

Rushkoff maintains that, when we are using social media sites, we are no longer in charge of our online identities or of the network of relations connected to us, and consequently, the company is able to exploit the information we implicitly and explicitly provide to produce revenue.

In the following passages, I focus on how Facebook in 2011 experimented with automation of sharing and activation of participation to build more affective encounters with the platform. Instead of Sponsored Stories, I focus on how Facebook introduced two interconnected features: their Timeline user interface and the Open Graph protocol. Automation of participation, I argue through these materials, operates beyond advertising and is part of how the platform establishes conditions that activate users and invite them to participate.

Timeline

On September 22, 2011, Facebook introduced an update to the user interface named the Timeline. Facebook Help Center explains that the Timeline is "your collection of the photos, stories, and experiences that tell your story."[8] It is a visual archive that collects and displays an individual's previous posts, updates, and events in chronological order. It sorts these actions, puts them in the right places, and stores them for the future. This is emphasized on Facebook's official blog: "With Timeline, now you have a home for all the great stories you've already shared. They don't just vanish as you add new stuff."[9] Finding events, updates, and posts from the past is made easier in comparison to the previous interface, which provided no options other than browsing profile updates by continuously clicking backward through a number of posts. The user can now browse her Timeline through years and dates, filling in blanks by going back in time and adding events, even those that took place prior to her having joined Facebook. Timeline marks a user's birthday by default, and Facebook's official blog tells us, "Now, you and your friends will finally be able to tell all the different parts of your story—from the small things you do each day to your biggest moments."[10]

The Timeline is a Facebook feature designed to occupy what Brian Massumi calls "the emergent level of the world's movements."[11] Its birth is part of a larger capitalization of culture, the cultural industry, and labor defined by capitalism in the age of social media and networks.[12] It is a limit between participation and data, visible and invisible, user and platform. Timeline's infrastructure is highly dependent not only on users and the content users produce but also on the ways to manage and regulate their participation. Facebook conditions not only what can be shared but how that sharing takes place; links, photos, likes, and status updates have their specific role and function on the platform. Interfaces, as Ben Light notes, are not only visual but also political guides; they do politics with us and invite us to the process of participation by providing visual cues and suggestive taglines, such as "What's on your mind?"[13]

Facebook as media technology affords and enables certain activities instead of others.[14] The idea that users in digital networks operate in particular conditions, and are even exploited by them, is of course nothing new. "Users are *created* by 'using' in a similar manner to the way drug users are created by the drugs they (ab)use," Wendy Hui Kyong Chun, for example, maintains when discussing internet users.[15] This statement is less about the internet being addictive for individuals and more about the overall "structure of using while being used."[16] As is commonly noted, Facebook is free for its users; but instead of money, users "pay" for the use of Facebook by providing it data about their social relationships. Tracking and monitoring the user around the Web and wherever she goes by using, for instance, cookies and IP addresses[17] seems like a common practice nowadays. Social relationships are turned into value and financial capital through advertisement and marketing mechanisms, which are then pushed back to the users as different kinds of relationships.

In the case of social media, Maurizio Lazzarato's claim that a thing can only have economic value if it produces a social relationship seems to hold.[18] For instance, by looking at the prospectus given before the firm's 2012 IPO, we can see that value on Facebook is produced, distributed, extracted, claimed, and performed in three intertwined ways that all relate to users and their relationships not only with each other but also with developers, advertisers, and marketers.[19] First, value is extracted from people and turned into financial capital. For instance, Facebook offers advertisers "the ability to include 'social context' with their marketing messages. Social context is information that highlights a user's friends' connections with a particular brand or business, for example, that a friend Liked a product or checked in at a restaurant."[20] Second, Facebook is valuable to its users in ways that exceed the economic definition of value. The platform lets users express themselves, connect with friends, and stay connected "wherever they go."[21] Third, value is tied to social relations that can be extrapolated into relationships of innovation, production, and consumption. Developers can create "products that are personalized and social and that offer new ways for our users to engage with friends and share experiences across the web and on mobile devices. For example, a Facebook user can visit the Pandora website and immediately begin listening to a personalized radio station that is customized based on the bands the user Likes on Facebook."[22] Things can have economic value if they produce a social relationship, but social relationships can themselves be produced as well.

The Timeline, of course, is not framed by Facebook as a technology that brings the company more financial capital by exploiting users. Rather, it is seen as empowering, giving users more control of their profiles. According to Facebook, the list of things one can do with Timeline is extensive. It is divided into three parts: cover, stories, and apps. The cover is a concise visual representation of the user that combines pictures, basic information, and details such as the number of one's Facebook friends. Stories include actions familiar to the user: she can edit personal information ranging from occupation to residence, view and add photos, and post status updates. Apps show users' app activity, for example, what music they listen to on Spotify or what they read on the *Washington Post* and other news sites. As Daniel Rosenberg and Anthony Grafton maintain, timelines connect to the processes of visualizing history, and they provide particular conditions of expression, which define how things such as history become known.[23] Timelines divide time and organize it into sequences.[24] Timelines control what can be seen and heard. The Facebook Timeline is an apparatus of power in a similar manner: it maps relations between forces.[25]

The power of the Timeline, I argue, relates to how it organizes participation. To understand the change that is implicated in its operation, a quick recap on how participation in the context of Web 2.0 and social media studies has been previously defined is in order. User participation became the key way to understand our relationships in the new media landscape filled with Wikipedia and YouTube, for example. One of the most visible, and most clichéd, marks of this boom was *Time* magazine's 2006 choice of "You" as the person of the year, with "You" referring to the vast and ever-growing group of web users who contributed to user-generated content across different web platforms. The centrality of user production permeated network culture from arts to sciences, from businesses and leisure to work. Henry Jenkins coined the idea of participatory culture to contrast the notions of passive media spectatorship and introduced new forms of participation and collaboration.[26] Emerging alongside media convergence, participatory culture described how users were in new ways engaged with media consumption processes. Transmedia storytelling introduced narratives that operated across media channels. The vibrant fan communities participated by writing fan fiction that emerged where other cultural products, such as movies, ended. Users were encouraged to generate content for a video game, for example. New forms of participation and collaboration were forged, and users became engaged with social media. For Jenkins, the occurrences of participatory culture indicated a huge potential for user autonomy.[27]

The moment of participatory culture celebrated users and their almost omnipotent capabilities enabled by connections in networked society. The user model of social media indicated a change in the industrial models of production where the chain of actors was traditionally divided into three distinct operators: producers, distributors, and consumers. Web 2.0 blurred the lines between these three actors and brought along hybrid user–producer–consumer models. These user subjects not only utilized existing resources but also produced new resources while participating. A number of authors from Yochai Benkler to Jenkins to Axel Bruns saw the change in the models of production as a positive move.[28] The most optimistic writers noted that the network culture was a potential platform for "individual freedom," "democratic participation," and "a medium to foster more critical and self-reflexive culture."[29] More discrete notions were also put forward that emphasized the fact that this new user model is an alternative to, for example, the mechanisms of industrial production of content, knowledge, and information. They indicate that a change in the modes of production is possible through new technologically mediated means.[30]

Soon also more critical notions of the conditions according to which participation is enabled emerged. Mirko Tobias Schäfer argues that user participation in social media can be divided into categories of the explicit and the implicit. Motivation drives explicit participation and includes different content-providing activities, such as sharing photos, participating in discussions, and liking things.[31] This is the mode of participation where the previous discussions of participatory culture had been focusing. The more critical takes, by, for example, Schäfer, pointed out that the data users provided while communicating and interacting in social media were also shared implicitly.[32] Implicit participation benefits from explicit participation but "does not necessarily require a conscious activity of cultural production."[33] Instead, implicit participation means tracking information from user activities performed on social media platforms and using this information for different purposes. On the level of the interface, the Timeline is situated somewhere along a continuum running between the categories of explicit and implicit user participation. Its visual design is based on user-generated content, such as photos and posts, but simultaneously, it becomes the organizer of implicit participation in the sense that, for example, apps used or pages liked become stored there automatically.

When Schäfer discusses implicit participation, he is addressing less how the interface visualizes this information and more how, for example, implicit participation is utilized in targeted advertising or software and platform design. The line between consumers and producers is blurred, and forms of labor are transformed.[34] Implicit participation in particular involves "unacknowledged" labor or "unconsciously performed" labor.[35] On one hand, digital labor increases creativity, produces new cultural inventions, and helps people solve problems in large groups. On the other hand, the content created and the digital labor used to create it become means of exploitation. "Besides uploading content, users also willingly and unknowingly provide important information about their profile and behaviour to site owners and metadata aggregators," Jose van Dijck argues.[36] Critical social media research often highlights the importance of implicit participation. Robert W. Gehl argues that social media users are immaterial laborers whose content production and affect are turned into marketing data.[37] Rushkoff gives us an even more pessimistic view of user participation social media: "The true end users of Facebook are the marketers who want to reach and influence us. They are Facebook's paying customers; we are the product. And we are its workers. The countless hours that we—and the young, particularly—spend on our profiles are the unpaid labor on which Facebook justifies its stock valuation."[38]

Although *implicit* and *explicit* participation are suitable terms to describe what is or can be shared, as forms of categorization, they do not exhaustively explain why we participate in social networks. This is the emergent level of participation—level where it becomes active. The activation of participation is the surplus that becomes produced in between explicit and implicit participation. Massumi names this "surplus-value of flow" and talks about a "movement-effect," a loop in which mining of data is utilized to create new products, which again produce new data and new products.[39] In other words, while for the user data have use value (e.g., data as content in the form of photos visualizing a user's Timeline) and for the platform exchange value (data as a commodity for advertisers), these dynamics are also designed to activate future participation (which then produces more content and more data). In the context of Timeline, the surplus manifests as the potential for clicks, actions, and interactions. A photo on a Timeline does not only visualize or tell a story but can be liked, commented, and shared. Activation of participation is produced through specific mechanisms. Future participation is embodied in the functions of Facebook's interface and the ways in which the Like and Share buttons are reworking different Web pages into Facebook-compatible objects, as Carolin Gerlitz and Anne Helmond have noted.[40] The affectivity of likes, recommendations, and activities, the capitalization of the potentiality of social activities, has a central position in this process. Almost anything that is incorporable into Facebook can generate a new click.

Happy Accidents

The discussion of Timeline suggests two interrelated questions concerning value production. The first is the well-discussed question of how to multiply the users' possibilities for content production and track and mine information provided by them.[41] Equally important but less discussed is the question I am addressing here: how to produce more clicks, more actions, and more interactions on social media platforms. What makes us tick parallels the equally compelling question, what makes us click?

If we are to believe Rushkoff, Facebook is programming us and reducing our spontaneity,[42] and if we use its interface and like things, we are losing control of ourselves and what is being marketed with our online profiles.[43] Activation of participation is a question of agency and affect. What is important here is the very material reading of Facebook's interface as that which enables certain things and disables others. Affect, if we follow Brian Massumi, "is a real condition, an intrinsic variable of the late capitalist system, as infrastructural as a factory."[44] Social media sites build on what Massumi calls "the ability of affect to produce an economic effect more swiftly and surely than economics itself."[45] Affect generates participation, and participation generates affective encounters.

From this perspective, a closer look into Facebook's interface and its features is in order. Along the Timeline, Zuckerberg announced that Facebook had been expanding the Open Graph protocol, which would help users connect anything, such as communications, games and media, and lifestyle applications, to their Facebook experience.[46] Protocols such as the Open Graph, which is designed to integrate websites into the Facebook interface, are not merely technical systems that allow communication but also give rise to protocological articulations and assemblages; that is, they work and shape the platform and the surrounding world in specific ways.[47] Protocols are governed and programmed sets of technical, physical, and political rules that control and guide the network architecture and simultaneously build the horizon of potentialities for user participation.[48] To understand the Open Graph, it should be noted that since 2006, Facebook has been developing a principle called social graph, which, as Anne Helmond notes, maps "connections between people and objects, for building applications."[49] As an actual manifestation of this logic, the Open Graph was launched in 2010 and, according to Taina Bucher, "consisted of a protocol, an application programming interface (API) and social plugins, including the now ubiquitous 'Like' button."[50] While the previous version of the Open Graph was built around the Like button, the 2011 redesign of Open Graph was intended to make different websites and data objects more Facebook compatible, and in addition to liking things on Facebook, users would be able to express a range of more specific coded actions toward particular objects, such as reading and watching.[51]

On the outset, the Open Graph provides content for an individual's Timeline. It helps users track and express their lives on Facebook more thoroughly. It also enables the user to discover new things through Facebook friends. At the developer conference of 2011, we are introduced to three characteristics for the Open Graph: frictionless experience, real-time serendipity, and finding patterns. "Frictionless experience" refers, for example, to applications that publish things automatically to one's Timeline. The apps will not have to ask the user's permission to publish content on their Facebook site every time; the permission is given once on a specific screen. For example, *Mashable* in a news story about Open Graph applications describes that the users of the *Washington Post* Social Reader app can read stories without leaving Facebook, and "once the user reads an article, the activity is shared with friends and included in the Facebook ticker"; the application not only shows activity but also recommends content based on users' Facebook likes or what the users' friends have been reading.[52] Finding patterns and data is an important part of the Open Graph. According to Irina Kaldrack and Theo Röhle, for website owners, Open Graph "provides an infrastructure for the circulation of content and simultaneously lets them trace the paths that individual elements are taking, e.g. via sharing and commenting."[53] What is also produced through frictionless sharing is "real-time serendipity," a principle of finding posted things and interacting with them without leaving the Facebook interface. Open Graph is a key part of Facebook's mechanism, which turns everything into sharing and makes sharing feel frictionless and immediate, as Robert Payne notes.[54] Zuckerberg's example in the F8 presentation is music discovery: "you can listen to Spotify songs within Facebook, being able to click on someone's music and play it. When someone discovers a song you get a notification."[55] Stumbling upon a Facebook-compatible object set things into motion.

The automated actions that produce frictionless experience and real-time serendipity are essential for the activation of participation and constitute what I define here as a *happy accident*. Happy accidents are, for example, status updates, photos, posts, and music that the user stumbles upon when using Facebook. They are content that the user does not expect or search for but that is offered by the platform through its mechanisms. They are not always shared intentionally by other users but are extracted from user participation by the platform. Accidents, following Paul Virilio, are always essential parts of any given technology; they give it shape and form.[56] In the context of Open Graph, accidents are produced to surprise the user and reveal something that would otherwise remain hidden. Yet, these happy accidents are hardly accidental; rather, they are based on patterns and data. Happy accidents, thus, are part of what Bucher defines as Facebook's automated attention management, where user attention is not only captured but always also anticipated.[57] Also, if these accidents are "happy," they are so in the sense that Sara Ahmed describes happy objects: "happiness functions as a promise that directs us toward certain objects, which then circulate as social goods."[58] Happy accidents imply a relatively passive user, a follower who accidently stumbles upon things and is then activated by them. With happy accidents, Facebook produces an affective feeling of the randomness of discovery, which can become contagious through the platform's features, such as liking, commenting, or sharing. "Faced with an algorithmically sorted social networking system like Facebook, users do not merely browse the content that *they* find interesting; the 'interesting' content increasingly finds them," as Bucher puts it.[59]

These streams and flows of objects constitute Facebook's intangible assets[60] and are essential to producing value for users. These flows manifest the promise of a happy accident: that there is always something interesting to find on Facebook, that every time one logs on, one might stumble upon something unique and original, unseen and interesting—something affective. This also engages users in the loops of participation; your friend might also find the thing you liked, shared, or did affective and become affected by it.

Indeed, as Jennifer Pybus maintains, the production of affect is at the very core of social media operations, which rely on the double axis of social participation and data mining.[61] Affect is that which makes us do or not do certain things, as Skeggs and Wood highlight.[62] For Pybus, affect is that which grounds our experiences of the surrounding world.[63] Affect, then, operates in the present moment. It extends toward possible actions, ideas, and emotions. It is present in every situation as potentiality, as the virtual possibility of encountering and experiencing something that only later can be manifested in words and emotions, or, in the language of Facebook, in clicks and recommendations.

The potentiality of affect has a central position in Deleuze's reading of Spinoza.[64] Deleuze maintains that the body is an assemblage of force relations and that the power of being affected determines how such assemblages may take place. Bodies are formed in the processes of affecting and being affected. According to Massumi, the transaction that alters bodies' capabilities takes place during moments of affection:

> When you affect something, you are at the same time opening
> yourself up to being affected in turn, and in a slightly different way
> than you might have been the moment before. You have made a

transition, however slight. You have stepped over a threshold. Affect is this passing of a threshold, seen from the point of view of the change in capacity.[65]

Affects interfere with our sensing, thinking, and acting; on Facebook, they offer us different connections and new modes of connectivity. This is how happy accidents work. The feeling that the content that appears on Facebook's different streams and feeds is serendipitous or frictionless is produced in the back end in order to affect. Opening a threshold is Open Graph's central mode of operation. It creates points where a double orientation of data production and affect generation takes place. In a most concrete sense, these points are Facebook-compatible objects managed by the protocol and automatically posted on users' feeds and streams. Thus the value of happy accidents could be understood in terms of Gabriel Tarde's economic psychology rather than by Marxian economics.[66] In other words, it is a question of how ideas, beliefs, and desires can move from individual to individual, not necessarily voluntarily through active participation but following the logic of contamination and contagion, and how technologies such as social media platforms boost and extend these processes.[67]

Applications

In 2011, the Open Graph protocol was introduced, following Alexander Galloway's definition of a protocol, to regulate on Facebook "how specific technologies are agreed to, adopted, implemented, and ultimately used by people around the world."[68] While Facebook has algorithmic methods of, for example, deciding what content will be shown on individual Facebook users' News Feeds at a given time,[69] the Open Graph of 2011 was an experiment of how different content can become part of Facebook's platform in the first place. As the Facebook developer site in 2012 puts it, the Open Graph includes "arbitrary actions and objects created by third party apps and enabling these apps to integrate deeply into the Facebook experience."[70] The Open Graph is a Facebook-specific mechanism to fold things within the platform through applications, or "apps," as the term is often shortened.

The *Washington Post* Social Reader of 2011 is an example of an app that tailors news content based on users' likes and interests. More important, it automatically shares the stories read on *Washington Post* with one's Facebook friends. "The Washington Post Social Reader is a way for people to connect around the day's latest happenings and discover real-time news with their friends on Facebook," says Donald Graham, chairman and CEO of the Washington Post company.[71]

According to the Facebook developer site, applications are a way for the users to express themselves, and these actions can be displayed on the user's Timeline, Ticker, and News Feed:

> The Open Graph allows apps to model user activities based on actions and objects. A running app may define the ability to "run" (action) a "route" (object). A reading app may define the ability to "read" (action) a "book" (object). A recipe app may define the ability to "cook" (action) a "recipe" (object). Actions are verbs that users perform in your app. Objects define nouns that the actions apply to. We created sets of actions and objects for common use cases and a tool for you to create your own custom actions and objects.[72]

Open Graph's purpose was to create Facebook-compatible objects that an individual can then deploy. As usage gets posted to an individual's Facebook page, the object becomes visible and potentially affective, thereby attracting new interactions. You can "read" a "book" on Facebook, where "reading" is an action and "book" is an object defined and categorized by the platform and the developer. "As users engage with your app, social activities are published to Facebook which connects the user with your objects, via the action," the Facebook Developer site maintains, and with the "open graph," the description continues, "your app becomes a part of the user's identity and social graph." In other words, when actions are published, they can appear on different places on Facebook—not only on your Timeline or your News Feeds but also on your friends' News Feeds and Ticker windows.[73] When participation becomes automated, user agency also becomes intertwined with the platform's nonhuman agency—we do not have to share content voluntarily to participate; rather, sharing and participation become a feature of the platform.

José van Dijck maintains that "user agency . . . encompasses a range of different uses and agents, and it is extremely relevant to develop a more nuanced model of understanding its cultural complexity."[74]

Indeed, focusing on the human subject and their participation seems to undermine the role of other actors involved in the generation and circulation of affect. Jane Bennett argues that we need to consider more thoroughly the participation of nonhuman material in everyday events.[75] For Bennett, all actors, even nonhuman ones, are social in the sense that they are bodies with a capability to affect and be affected.[76] A similar understanding of affect and affectivity can be traced from Spinoza to Deleuze to Massumi. Deleuze and Guattari, for example, address bodies in a nonhuman sense when they maintain that

> we know nothing about a body until we know what it can do, in other words, what its affects are, how they can or cannot enter into composition with other affects, with the affects of another body, either to destroy that body or to be destroyed by it, either to exchange actions and passions with it or to join with it in composing a more powerful body.[77]

Expanding the focus to include nonhuman operators is necessary to understand what Bennett calls impersonal affect, that is, affect that is not "transpersonal" or "intersubjective" but "intrinsic to forms that cannot be imagined . . . as persons."[78] Impersonal affect, then, points to a body as a composition that does not have essentialist features but is formed as an assemblage.

Interestingly, however, while Bennett argues that impersonal affect is intrinsic to a form that cannot be imagined as a person, we see a reverse operation in the case of Timeline. In his book *Present Shock* (2013), Rushkoff notes, "Even though we may be able to be in only one place at a time our digital selves are distributed across every device, platform, and network onto which we have cloned our virtual identities."[79] The Facebook Timeline does its best to transform impersonal affect into something imagined as persons (hence also Facebook's one-user-account and real-name policies). It is always the named user who has done something, who has liked something, who has listened to something. This does not mean that the named user, however, is a person or even will become a person. On the contrary, named users are nonhuman and human compositions that appear personlike but cluster around impersonal affects. The same could be said about the *Washington Post* Social Reader. What Graham calls "social reading" or "social news"[80] is an automated and platform-produced mode of sociality where the lines not only between automation and participation but also between the individual and the platform are blurred to produce a happy accident.

The impersonal affect functions differently in Facebook's different streams and feeds. According to Facebook Social Design, Open Graph uses third-party apps to include "arbitrary actions and objects" in the Facebook experience.[81] As the Facebook developer page puts it:

> after a user adds your app to their Timeline, app specific actions are shared on Facebook via the Open Graph. As your app becomes an important part of how users express themselves, these actions are more prominently displayed throughout the Facebook Timeline, News Feed, and Ticker. This enables your app to become a key part of the user's and their friend's experience on Facebook.[82]

Timeline, News Feed, and Ticker form the core visible infrastructure of Facebook's impersonal streams of affect, which then are used by the applications. While the Timeline is the archive of one's content, the News Feed is an endlessly updating stream of content provided by named Facebook users, advertisers, and liked pages. News Feed is what the user first sees when they access their Facebook account. After the Open Graph implementation, not all the content visible in the News Feed is created by the users. Sometimes applications themselves can be authorized to post on News Feed. To post autonomously on behalf of the user, applications need only request publishing permissions for "publish_stream" and "publish_actions."[83] The latter permission is used, for example, by games to automatically post high scores on an individual's Timeline. While they relate to a person, the affects they are intended to generate are impersonal. As much as they indicate what the particular individual user is doing, they also indicate what is possible to do on Facebook.

Whereas News Feed would portray users' important moments and Timeline store them, Ticker was planned to be a real-time continuous stream of information of what users' were doing on Facebook. When it was launched in 2011, Facebook's engineering manager Mark Tonkelowitz explained that "Ticker shows you the same stuff you were already seeing on Facebook, but it brings your conversations to life by displaying updates instantaneously. Now when a friend comments, asks a question or shares something like a check in, you'll be able to join the conversation right away. Click on anything in ticker to see the full story and chime in—without losing your place."[84] Through Ticker, user actions become visible to other users. A variation of News Feed, Ticker displays a real-time stream of friends' activities. While News Feed shows the actual things shared, Ticker shares what becomes actualized as clicks, likes, and comments. When clicking on a post on Ticker, one can see conversations on friends' walls as well as photos posted by total strangers on which one's friends have commented. Similarly, activities like listening to music can be translated into social and clickable experiences through applications. For example, and to recap, Spotify can be integrated with Facebook so that the music to which a user listens appears in the News Feed, on Ticker, and on its own section in Timeline. Other users can click on the track and start playing the same music. This information is also then posted to their News Feed, Ticker, and Timeline streams. The Spotify integration generates an affective experience of music even when not audible. According to Facebook's blog, Spotify represents a new kind of social app "that lets you show the things you like to do on your Timeline—the music you listen to, the recipes you try, the runs you take and more."[85] Arguably, however, the user is not showing anything, for it is the app itself that exposes the user and translates her music preferences into impersonal affects. The music played becomes a part of an affective flow that potentially attracts new users. Ticker is automatic. It extracts affect from user actions. With Ticker, the personal becomes impersonal and the impersonal becomes affects. If social media sites run "coded protocols that appear to 'mediate' people's social activities, while in fact *steering* social traffic," as van Dijck notes, News Feed and Ticker seem to fit with this description quite well.[86] These feeds and streams affect users' experiences on social media. While there is a sensation of experiencing what users do online, it is also Facebook that regulates what processes become visible. This selection happens "hidden behind the screen's features."[87] This harnessing of the power of affect that, on behalf of the user, emerges automatically, unintentionally, and uncontrolledly may be regarded as one of the biggest experiments in the 2011 Facebook interface renewal.

Consequently, when Graham of the *Washington Post* discussed their Social Reader Facebook app in 2011, he was quite optimistic, mentioning that "this is part of the future of news" and that "we're trying to get the product right. We're trying to get market share. We're trying to see how big we can make it."[88] Ironically, only about a year later, in December 2012, the *Washington Post,* along with the *Guardian,* decided to remove its social reader from Facebook. According to the news reports of the time, the monthly user amounts of these social reading apps declined radically, the users complained about privacy settings, and the automated sharing function didn't seem personal but rather forced and impersonal.[89] A story in *Adweek* doomed frictionless sharing as a mistake, claiming that the automated sharing function of the Open Graph was exploited by different applications to grow the user base and fill users' Facebook feeds with content they didn't in some cases realize they were sharing.[90] According to the same story, Facebook tried to adjust its platform to stop "bad surprises," but in the end, users stopped adding Facebook apps because they did not want to feel "spammy."[91] On December 1, 2017, Facebook notified that they had also finally removed the Ticker feature.[92] While many of the visible functions may have changed, the Open Graph itself has not disappeared. Its core function to turn any website Facebook compatible for sharing still remains.

What the Open Graph renewal of 2011 together with the principle of frictionless and serendipitous experience was meant to create is what Kaldrack and Röhle call "a space of co-presence, which simulates shared presence and promises participation."[93] This experience, which was based on automating participation and, for example, sharing on a user's own Facebook feeds the content the user browsed on outside sources, was perhaps too much in-your-face. Happy accidents may generate frictionless and serendipitous experiences when they manifest on the interface as status updates, likes, even advertisements, but their production also always connects to what happens under the hood. The automated sharing appearing on Ticker and News Feed and published by apps on Timeline on a user's behalf made the nonhuman agency of social media too visible. Users voted by disconnecting the apps and stopped using them. Facebook stopped using the word "frictionless" to describe the user experience.[94]

While many of the visible functions may have changed, happy accident as a principle and the Open Graph as a method of organizing content are still there. With the Open Graph, users can still utilize apps to "use stories to share the things they're doing, the people they're doing them with and the places where they happen."[95] Kaldrack and Röhle point out that what the Open Graph established was tools for a network analysis of the value of nodes or node associations and statistical methods to assert "similarities, normalities or deviations, focusing on the features of actors."[96] Open Graph was a technology to organize and produce valuable information, not only to users in the form of happy accidents but also for the platform.[97] Hence maybe what was important about the protocol was always that which was implicit and remained unseen, of which the happy accidents gave us an explicit glimpse. That is, every song you listen to, every website you browse, every online news article you read, every place you visit, the people you interact with, when connected to Facebook's platform are visible for the site and can find different forms at the levels of affective flow.

Coda

In 2016, three years after Rushkoff left Facebook, Ian Tucker, a reporter for the *Guardian,* interviewed him, asking how the abstention has worked.[98] While Rushkoff is ready to see some professional benefits to being on social media, the fundamental problem for him is still that the platforms hide their operations and adhere to the logic of marketing. As Ilana Gershon maintains, Facebook profiles have been understood as intrinsically linked to users' offline lives and as representations of embodied selves created by the password holders from the choices Facebook provides.[99] The production of happy accidents gives us a different view. It shows that the questions of user identity and subjectivity on social media are always also questions of bodies' capabilities to affect and be affected by and on the platform through the features and functions of both. Rushkoff gives us a dystopic understanding of what Facebook users are for the company: "they [Facebook] can use your face and name to advertise through you, that's what you've agreed to. I didn't want Facebook to advertise something through me as an influencer where my every act becomes grist to marketing."[100] Facebook's launch of the Timeline and expansion of the Open Graph protocol in 2011 exemplify some of Rushkoff's concerns. Happy accidents retain a promise that the user will find something interesting shared by their peer every time the user logs on. But this also

means that happy accidents need to be produced by any means necessary. The peer needs to produce. The *Washington Post* Social Reader
and other similar apps, were Facebook's platform-specific mechanisms
designed to automate participation and sharing to produce happy accidents. They were automated answers to the question of how to make
users participate. When we sign up and log in for social media, we
become susceptible to happy accidents, but we also participate in their
production explicitly and implicitly. Happy accidents exemplify, paraphrasing Susanna Paasonen, that social media users may have agency,
but this agency is far from autonomous.[101]

Deactivate

Everyone now wants to know how to remove themselves from
social networks. It has become absolutely clear that our relationships to others are mere points in the aggregation of marketing
data. Political campaigns, the sale of commodities, the promotion
of entertainment—this is the outcome of our expression of likes
and affinities.[1]

These are the opening words of the "Facebook Suicide Bomb Manifesto," which urges Facebook users to reclaim their lives and leave
social networks by committing a digital suicide attack. The manifesto
was written by Sean Dockray and first published on the iDC mailing
list on May 28, 2010. The "Facebook Suicide Bomb Manifesto" is part
of a phenomenon that is mapped in this chapter under the notion of
digital suicide. It is connected to notions like *digital detox* and *digital fast*. *Detox* and *fast* can, on one hand, refer to modes of political
asceticism used to resist the time-consuming and capitalistic modes
of production associated with social media; on the other hand, they
implicate that social media have the capacity to turn users into what
Félix Guattari calls "machinic junkies" or "machinic subjectivities."[2]

According to Guattari, "everything that contributes to provide
a sensation of belonging to something, of being somewhere, along
with the sensation of forgetting oneself, are 'drugs.'"[3] The sense of
being and belonging is created by social media platforms through two
axes: on one hand, they make the platform personal by inviting users
into a process of curating their lives through adding information and

establishing contacts with each other; on the other, through a mechanic process of repetition, such as liking, commenting, lurking, and retweeting, they produce habits, which, as Wendy Hui Kyong Chun describes, are voluntary and involuntary, conscious and automatic, at the same time.[4] Users in this scheme become machinic subjectivities whose identities are individuated according to preestablished categories like age, profession, or gender, for instance, and at the same time, these networks work on a level prior to any ready-made categories and identities structuring the flows of sensations, affects, and relations that are not yet individuated.[5]

Popular social media platforms are also businesses, and the production of machinic subjectivities is tied to the political economy of the platform.[6] Social media sites and their ways to capitalize on users are constantly evolving. Social media platforms and their business models are constantly developing means of governing bodies, objects, and data for the sake of profit. New forms of commodities and commodity relations are built. Users are turned into consumers, and they are involved in the act of consumption through sharing, collecting, experiencing, and, as proposed by Nigel Thrift, "in general, participating in all manner of collective acts of sensemaking."[7] Users' subjectivity is both inserted into incorporeal networks and produced and exploited by them.[8]

Gary Genosko, following Guattari, calls this wired consumerism and argues that it requires "detox by disconnection."[9] This chapter looks into the consumerism of social media platforms through different media artworks of digital suicide that abstain the user from particular social media sites. These artworks can be roughly divided into two categories: software-based artworks that automate the processes of leaving and artworks that are confessional and instructive, where artists turn their own digital suicide as a performance. The former are *Seppukoo.com* by the Les Liens Invisibles and *Web 2.0 Suicide Machine* by moddr_, both from 2009, and the latter are Man Bartlett's *I Deleted My Facebook Account* from 2012 and *Digital Suicide* by Liam Scully, exhibited in 2015. The fifth work, Nik Briz's *How to/ Why Leave Facebook (on My Own Terms, without "Deleting" My Account)* from 2014, is located somewhere in the middle. These works are used to address the problems of being engaged with social media platforms through the productive acts of disconnecting. Bartlett made a performance of his process of leaving the site, inviting people to participate. Briz created an instructional site where he guides the user in deleting her Facebook site through ways that are not implemented by Facebook. And Scully's work is composed of drawings based on the data he was able to download from Facebook when he deleted his user account. *Seppukoo.com* and *Web 2.0 Suicide Machine* place the emphasis on the platform political side of our social media engagements. They are targeted at and exploit the operations of specific platforms; *Web 2.0 Suicide Machine* disconnects Facebook, MySpace, Twitter, and LinkedIn accounts, while *Seppukoo.com* is designed to disconnect the user from Facebook. These works, through the lens of disconnection, address how life from social relations to economy to interests is tied into social media and driven through the mechanisms and changes taking place on the platforms. They are tactical media in the sense that by interfering, they illustrate the complex chains of political, economic, and even legal questions to which digital suicide gives birth and the deep structures of our contemporary digital culture, which the predominant discourses of social media hype sometimes hides.

It is the commercial culture coded within the platform that digital suicide contests. To rephrase, digital suicide aims not to end "life" but to separate it from the "economics" and "politics" of social media platforms. Thus the theoretical basis for analyzing digital suicide is found in Michel Foucault's concept of biopolitics developed in his lectures at the Collège de France from 1975 to 1976.[10] Although there have been various interpretations of biopolitics, I will follow Alexander Galloway and Eugene Thacker's suggestion to use the concept in a very specific manner: as biopolitics of the network culture.[11]

Framing Digital Suicide

While digital suicide and works such as *Seppukoo.com* and *Web 2.0 Suicide Machine,* along with "Facebook Suicide Bomb Manifesto," gained much attention in the media, this was not the first time avant-garde art adopted suicide to reveal underlying mechanisms of current society. Mapping the media archaeological traces of suicide machines, we can point out few illustrative examples. The idea of a suicide machine was already present in the *(Unspeakable) Ultimate Machine* built by Claude Shannon in the 1950s. Friedrich Kittler tells us the story:

> As a young student at MIT, Shannon is said to have built the
> simplest, most elegant and most useless of all digital machines. It
> boasted one single ON/OFF switch. Whenever Shannon's friends
> came to visit, the machine was on OFF. Sometimes, when they were
> in a playful mood, the visitors switched it to ON. Whereupon the
> lid of the machine opened, a hand appeared, fumbled around for
> the switch, put it on OFF again and disappeared under the closing
> lid.[12]

The *Ultimate Machine* was a simple wooden box with a switch on
the side. When the switch was turned on, the lid of the box opened
and a mechanical hand reached from the box to turn off the switch.
Subsequently, the hand retracted back inside the box, leaving the box
in its initial state. The *Ultimate Machine* worked with Boolean logic,
having only two possible values of "on" and "off."

Another example is the case of the Luther Blissett Project, one of
the most famous cases of committing a virtual suicide. In 1994, Luther
Blissett became a multiple-use name (a nom de plume) for a number
of artists and activists around Europe. It was an open network, but
its core was in Bologna, Italy, where a group of people had based the
project. Numerous pranks were conducted under the name of Luther
Blissett, some trying to show the problems prevailing in the cultural
ambience and others just for the sake of exploiting the gullibility of the
press and people.[13] The project was planned to have a five-year cycle,
and in 1999, it had reached the end. It was, however, not taken down
quietly. In a letter dated September 6, 1999, the Luther Blissett Project
announced that they would commit seppuku, a formal Japanese ritual
suicide that was often performed in front of spectators. Did the people
behind Luther Blissett kill themselves? Most certainly not, but they
made a ritual performance out of the abandonment of their multiple-
use name identity. The pseudonym Luther Blissett was not to be used
by the project anymore. The seppuku of Luther Blissett was in essence
a virtual suicide. But as the project members state, it was not an act
of relinquishment or nihilism; instead, they were choosing life. It was
said to be a birth of something new.[14]

One of the first actual digital suicide attempts was by the artist
Cory Arcangel, when, in December 2005, he decided to delete his
Friendster account as part of the launch of the December/January

issue of *The Believer* magazine. He called it a "Friendster Suicide." Arcangel explained his urge for digital suicide with both personal reasons, saying that he "just can't take it [Friendster] anymore," and performative reasons, inviting people to watch him do it online.[15] Similar self-conscious projects are carried on even now. For example, *Delete Your Account,* established in 2015, is an initiative by curators Willa Köerner and Alex Teplitzky that is both a blog and also an event of reading, performing, and media sharing one's own posting that one "should probably delete from the internet."[16]

More political digital suicide projects emerged in the late 2000s. They were targeted toward social networks making profits with their users and shared content and exploiting real friend networks for commercial means. For example, MyOwnspace.fr published an Anti-MySpace Banner Wizard for users of MySpace. It declared, "Good Karma: suicide yourself . . . from MySpace." The idea was that users would leave a site like MySpace, which aimed to make profit from its users, and join profit-free sites like MyOwnspace.[17]

These previous cases of suicide technology contributed directly or indirectly to the emergence of digital suicide in the early 2010s. The aforementioned works by Bartlett, Briz, and Scully carry on the more individual and personal trends of digital suicide preceded by Cory Arcangel, for example. But they were also created as responses to different political problems Facebook has generated. Bartlett decided to create his digital suicide artwork when Facebook in 2012 changed users' default email addresses in their bios to facebook.com email address. Choosing users' default email addresses indicated for Bartlett not a violation of privacy but an exercise of control over the individual by the platform.[18] Briz created his work as an intervention against Facebook's marketing mechanisms, which turn Facebook "likes" into advertising.[19] And finally, Scully's work was inspired by the 2013 Edward Snowden revelations and the potential for us, as social media users, to be part of mass surveillance.[20]

Both *Seppukoo.com*[21] by Les Liens Invisibles, presented in November 2009 during the Turin Share festival, and *Web 2.0 Suicide Machine*[22] by moddr_, presented in December 2009 at Rotterdam's Worm exhibition, follow more along the lines of the *(Unspeakable) Ultimate Machine* or Anti-MySpace Banner Wizard. They rely on the vulnerability of social media, the Facebook platform, in particular, and exploit their practices and processes of logging in and deactivating accounts. Both artworks and the groups behind them also have open ambitions to expose and reveal fallacies and problems in digital culture via art. Paraphrasing their own description, the Les Liens Invisibles, which is an Italy-based artist duo comprising Clemente Pestelli and Gionatan Quintini, has been "infiltrating the global communication networks in order to join and expand the invisible connections between art the mediascape and real life."[23] Moddr_, on the other hand, is run by a group of alumni from the Media Design MA course, and their practices involve modification (modding) and re-creation of already existing technologies; they state that their mission is to display a critical perspective on contemporary media that is labeled "new" through artistic practices.[24]

Since opening, both *Seppukoo.com* and *Web 2.0 Suicide Machine* have gained interest in the media and also captured the attention of social media businesses; according to letters from Facebook representatives, published on Seppukoo.com[25] and Suicidemachine.org,[26] Facebook took actions to stop these projects.[27] These letters indicate that the artworks were soliciting Facebook user login information, accessed Facebook accounts that belonged to others, scraped content from Facebook, and infringed on Facebook's intellectual property rights. These actions were demanded to be stopped immediately.[28] These cease-and-desist demands demonstrate how blurred the lines between media art, on one hand, and vandalism, sabotage, or illegal actions, on the other, can be. Action such as this, according to Jussi Parikka, is a common take on software art: it "is often not even recognized as 'art' but is defined more by the difficulty of pinning it down as social and cultural practices."[29]

If we build on the controversy of these works, we can deposit digital suicide and its manifestations in the realm of "bad objects"[30] or "evil media."[31] This is not to claim that these works are harmful (the Facebook view) or that they are emancipatory (the artist/activist view). Instead, I propose following Parikka and Sampson that we should look at the potentials of these works.[32] By way of illustration, this position means asking what kinds of connections they make and how they express and are expressed in network culture. These objects are not external to Facebook but instead are built and constructed with and partly within the site. Simultaneously, they reveal the role that digital networks play in human lives these days and how our lives are inter-connected with these networks to an extent that we can conceptualize our interactions with machines and technology with notions such as *life, death,* and *suicide.*

Biopolitics and Social Media Businesses

Digital suicide points to a larger theoretical field of life, death, and technology and their entanglements—what is living (and dying) in in-formation networks. Following Galloway and Thacker, we need to understand how networks structure our world.[33] For Galloway and Thacker, the basis for theory of the networks is to understand that net-works are not neutral or democratized per se but instead their forms of organization are in many ways politicized. From Michel Foucault, Galloway and Thacker borrow the concept of *biopolitics,* developed to address the modes of organizing, managing, and regulating an en-tity defined as the population.[34] There are three sides of biopolitics that are important for understanding social media connectivity. First, the object of biopolitics is the population. Second, population control can happen through modulation of an environment. Third, data and the production of data are the means through which the population–environment pair is understood and produced.

For Foucault, the governance of populations goes together with the governance of the environment or the milieu in which the people live.[35] Environments, for Foucault, can be natural or urban, and how they are shaped to shape life is crucial. One of Foucault's own ex-amples deals with the epidemics related to swamps in the nineteenth century; there was a relation between swamps and epidemics—if the swamps were dried out, the epidemics would also disappear.[36] Here we can think about media as environments and environments as media, as John Durham Peters notes.[37] Environments govern and can be governed. To think about social media through biopolitics, then, is to think about how they operate as an environment. Each social media site has its own peculiar modes of organization and power relations, which guide the movements of the user population.[38]

While culturing the nature may have been a solution for particular epidemics, turning the nature into cities brought its own problems; in another example, Foucault discusses how people overpopulated the cities and overpopulation caused the spread of diseases.[39] The new environment required new architectural and structural control methods, such as building ventilation systems. But there was also another change, where instead of specific individuals, the living conditions of the general population became the target of governance. What was introduced was governance through data, where different "forecasts, statistical estimates and overall measures" became the tools to "establish an equilibrium" or "maintain an average."[40] This gave rise to the different methods of producing data of the population and the implementation of these data into regulative purposes.

According to Galloway and Thacker, "biopolitics defines a means for the production of data surrounding its object (the population)."[41] Data and information, as we know, are essential also for social media platforms. José van Dijck sees social media users as content providers and data providers.[42] As an example of content and data produced, in *Digital Suicide,* Scully used Facebook's option to download all personal data into a single zip file when deleting one's user account to make multilayered drawings composed of pictures and Facebook conversations that took place between 2008 and 2013. Scully's work is focused on critically exposing the limits of data collection, and instead of life, reclaimed in this project are data. Or in other words, life has become data. With almost one thousand images, the work shows the extent of the data we voluntarily give out and expresses how layered these data are with texts, images, clicks, and likes.[43]

In its data policy, revised September 29, 2016, Facebook explains in detail what information is collected and how it is used. These data range from things a user does and shares to the information other people provide about the user to transactions the user makes to the devices they use and third-party apps and services connected to the site.[44] According to Facebook's data policy, the information one gives out is used to "provide and support" Facebook's services.[45] This means, for example, that the environment, the platform, can be constantly updated and modulated based on data gathered. Indeed, social media platforms need to adapt their designs and practices constantly according to changing situations, user interests, and preferences. Thus, instead of building a total system, social media platforms are in a constant state of being under construction and using data to anticipate what is yet to come.

This information is not only used by the company to build its platform but can also be shared with "advertising, measurement and analytics services" and with "vendors, service providers and other partners."[46] Support for the platform comes through monetization of data. In this scheme, users, as van Dijck also notes, have almost no power over their data distribution.[47]

When you bring your life, that is, social connections, political opinions, habits, and likes, into Facebook's environment, you simultaneously allow your life to become part of its business. Dimitry Kleiner and Brian Wyrick have, quite polemically, argued that "Web 2.0 is not to be thought of as a second-generation of either the technical or social development of the internet, but rather as the second wave of capitalist enclosure of the Information Commons."[48] Following the trend of ubiquitous or pervasive computing, everything is a potential node; everything from social relations to hobbies and interests are taken inside the network and transformed into commodities. Social media represent a business model in which user-created value is captured by a private enterprise.[49] In this biopolitical business model, social life becomes commodified, and hence the social becomes part of the economy instead of the economy being part of the social.[50] Internet security company F-Secure sums up these premises quite simply in its first tip for safer Facebooking: "Facebook is a business. It exists to take your online activity and turn it into revenue. Facebook will always be free. But there is a cost. You're paying by being exposed to advertising and allowing limited disclosure of your online activity."[51] As Parikka described and Sampson repeated, capital is a machine of capture trying to absorb everything inside its system—often successfully.[52]

Premediating Disconnection

The biopolitical system of social media is anticipatory. Different algorithms mine information, and coded operations predetermine which information is important for the user.[53] These algorithmic operations are parallel to biopolitical regulation mechanisms, which aim to control masses and predict, modify, and compensate for the effects of events affecting them.[54] Disconnection poses an ultimate challenge for both biopolitics and the capitalist system, because it means dropping out from the system of control.

Richard Grusin has described mediated actions of anticipating the future possibilities and reacting to them in advance with the concept of premediation.[55] For Grusin, premediation works in two senses. First, it produces specific future scenarios. Second, it creates continuity with present and future to maintain their connection and to exclude disruptions in the flow of daily lives. One example would be excluding disconnection. Producing potential scenarios of the future is a process where "the future is remediated at the very moment that it emerges into the present."[56] Grusin argues that through the ubiquity of interconnected media technologies, everything becomes premediated, from social relations to nonhuman objects and their interactions.

Laura Portwood-Stacer notes that Facebook tries to make itself ubiquitous so that we cannot even think about life without it.[57] Ben Light and Elijah Cassidy play with this idea, pointing out that "perhaps the most obvious point of engagement by Facebook in attempting to prevent termination is at the point when a user . . . tries to close their account."[58] In the following passages, I focus on the practices of leaving Facebook to give a few different examples of how premediation works as a design principle. For the user who wants to leave Facebook, three different choices are offered. The first one is simple and used daily by most of the basic users: logging out. This operation is enabled simply by clicking the account menu bar in the upper right corner of the Facebook page and selecting "Log Out." This throws the user out from the personal profile Facebook page back to the front page, where the user is able to sign in again. Quitting using the logout option on Facebook is not permanent. It is meant for users who do not want to leave their personal profile pages open for other users. This may be the case if someone is using a public computer, for example. If the user chooses not to log out but only closes the browser, the personal profile page opens directly without the necessity to log in the next time the user accesses her Facebook page with that browser. However, the logout feature does not actually equal quitting. The personal profile remains on Facebook. Logging out is just a method for temporarily breaking from the service.

A more drastic way to disconnect is to deactivate one's account. A Facebook user needs to click on the account menu, located in the upper right corner of the Facebook frame. From there, the user selects "Settings" and then, from the right-hand tab, "Security." The last selection there is "Deactivate Your Account." When the user chooses to deactivate, she is prompted to enter a password to continue. According to Facebook, "if you deactivate your account: You can reactivate whenever you want; People can't see your Timeline or search for you; Some info may remain visible (ex: messages you sent); We save your account info (ex: friends, interests), in case you reactivate."[59] To rephrase, what happens when you deactivate is that your personal profile page disappears. Your Facebook Timeline with your status updates and shared activities becomes invisible, and your friends can neither see you nor find you anymore. However, the user's personal profile does not disappear completely. Facebook saves the user's profile information so that if the user wants to reactivate the account at some point, it will look just the way it did when it was deactivated. All the friend connections are saved, and so is the content of the personal profile.

These two modes of quitting are easily accessed by the user. Both are found in the account settings menu, and neither appears hidden. There is, however, a third way to quit Facebook: the user is able to delete the Facebook account permanently. This means that all the content of the user's personal profile is removed permanently, including pictures, friends, Wall posts, and messages. This process is irreversible; there is no option for recovering the permanently deleted Facebook page. To delete an account, Facebook requests that the user contact them directly. The deletion, however, is not complete, because "some of the things you do on Facebook aren't stored in your account. For example, a friend may still have messages from you even after you delete your account. That information remains after you delete your account."[60]

The described modes of quitting Facebook show how premediation is not neutral but in fact tied into the subtle mechanisms of control. While there may be various ways of quitting Facebook, some of these possibilities are "encouraged by the protocols and reward systems built inside the game."[61] Control is not about creating an object that can be controlled but, for example, about anticipating the behavior of the users and reacting to that beforehand.[62] Indeed, although premediation condenses time and gives different future directions, it does not offer total freedom for the user nor total control over a user's choices but works somewhere in the middle, providing paths and links to follow and preferring some while pushing others back.

Maybe the most evident example that shows premediation in action happens when a person tries to deactivate his Facebook account. After choosing to deactivate the account, the user is guided to a page where he has to confirm the deactivation. This, of course, is nothing new. Quite simply, it is just a way to prevent accidental deactivation. However, the way the page is implemented is something remarkable. Not only is the present situation of choosing to confirm the disconnection mediated but also the future is premediated by showing a set of pictures of friends "who will miss you" after deactivating the account. Here premediation relies heavily on the affects created by profile pictures and names of the user's Facebook friends.

One cannot stress enough the importance of the posted image next to the profile pictures among friends who are said to miss the user after disconnection, because it leads to the logic of how Facebook works and also what many of the users who are afraid of losing their privacy dread: the content the users themselves create is used for different purposes that escape their original intentions. Entering into the time of premediation means also entering into a time of databases and data mining, where any datum may be accessed and used at any given point in time.[63] It is here where the machinic subjectivity of the user starts to unfold. Machinic subjectivities are Deleuze's "dividuals"; in social networks, we become codes, images, posts, that cannot be reduced to our offline presence.[64] We become doubles who exist simultaneously in different databases, information banks, and other technomaterial assemblages. As Genosko writes, "offline individual" is merely one actualization of the dividual, because "nobody totally corresponds to their data double or silhouette."[65] The catch is that after logging in to a social network service, there really is no return to the offline individuality. Even if a person deactivates her account, she remains in the databases of Facebook.

Digital Suicide: Environment

If our every action in Facebook is premediated and controlled by preemptive strategies, for which we ourselves provide the means by sharing content and information, how are we ever able to disconnect from these services? As discussed, even the ways of disconnecting leave not

Your friends will miss you if you deactivate your user account, Facebook warns us.

only backdoors open for returning to the service and reenabling social contacts with one simple click.

According to Rita Raley, in recent years, we have seen various direct responses to the rise of digital capitalism in the field of new media art, information art, and digital art.[66] With the concept of tactical media, she describes art forms that use practices like hacktivism, denial-of-service attacks, and reverse engineering. If there is a combining factor for these practices, it is the disturbance they create to the predominant environment within which they work. As Raley states, "in its most expansive articulation, tactical media signifies the intervention and disruption of a dominant semiotic regime, the temporary creation of a situation in which signs, messages, and narratives are set into play and critical thinking becomes possible."[67]

Bartlett's performance of leaving Facebook highlights the ephemerality of the process. He created a Facebook event for deleting his Facebook profile. Bartlett opened his own Facebook profile for modulation and has invited "anyone to spam my wall with their art, self-promotional info, dick pics or whatever they wanted."[68] For a short moment, the act of leaving becomes visible through the platform's own mechanisms.

Also, software-based works, such as *Seppukoo.com* and *Web 2.0 Suicide Machine*, take place with and on Facebook. Instead of being static art objects, they invite users inside a performative event. The bearing theme of *Seppukoo.com* and *Web 2.0 Suicide Machine* is reclaiming one's life through self-destructive actions in the digital world. *Seppukoo.com* seduces the Facebook user to commit a virtual suicide: "Discover what's after your facebook life. We assist your virtual identity suicide."[69] The same kind of rhetoric is also found from the description of *Web 2.0 Suicide Machine:* "Liberate your newbie friends with a Web2.0 suicide! This machine lets you delete all your energy sucking social-networking profiles, kill your fake virtual friends, and completely do away with your Web 2.0 alterego."[70]

What is important here is to understand that neither *Seppukoo.com* nor *Web 2.0 Suicide Machine* would exist without Facebook. Both of the services have specially emerged out of, and in direct response to, Facebook. This, however, does not mean that *Seppukoo.com* or *Web 2.0 Suicide Machine* is oppositional to Facebook. Quite the contrary, *Seppukoo.com* and *Web 2.0 Suicide Machine* operate within the parameters of Facebook. Following Galloway and Thacker, we could say that tactical media do not even want to change their target but instead find and exploit holes and security breaches inside the system and project potential changes through them.[71] In this sense, as also Raley observes, tactical media reshape the target, creating a temporary disturbance to the service instead of exiting the system entirely.[72] As Parikka argues, "resistance works immanently to the diagram of power and instead of refusing its strategies, it adopts them as part of its tactics."[73]

To elaborate this more thoroughly, we need to look at how *Seppukoo.com* and *Web 2.0 Suicide Machine* access user accounts in order to disconnect. It is the protocol of username and password through which both *Web 2.0 Suicide Machine* and *Seppukoo.com* infiltrate Facebook. The suicide starts by giving these sites Facebook usernames and passwords. In general, the password–username combination has become an order-word of network culture. Following Guattari, we can say that they give out stop and start orders but above all activate the "bringing into being of ontological Universes."[74] Passwords and usernames transmit the user from one line to another, from a service to another, from an identity to another. With password and username we enter into different web services, from Facebook to our banking services. According to Deleuze, passwords and codes define the key rules of control societies: "digital language of control is made up of codes indicating whether access to some information should be allowed or denied."[75]

Seppukoo.com uses the password to log on to the user's Facebook account and then uses his information to create a memorial page on the Seppukoo.com site. The user is able to choose a skin and utter last words that are shown on the memorial page. The last words and a testimony of committing suicide are sent to the user's Facebook friends. By using the viral strategies of contagion and distribution, *Seppukoo .com* aims to get more people to commit virtual suicide. The pièce de résistance of the social suicide is the game implemented in the experience. One gets points and raises their rank according to the number of Facebook friends who follow his lead and also commit *Seppukoo .com*. The memorial page shows friends who have committed suicide and friends who still are on Facebook.

Web 2.0 Suicide Machine, on the other hand, uses the password to cut the offline individual from Facebook permanently. It does this by changing the password—the user is no longer able to log in. Along with the password, the identity of the user is vacated to the software. Digital suicide is made irreversible. In addition, *Web 2.0 Suicide Machine* changes the profile picture of the user into the *Web 2.0 Suicide Machine*'s noose logo and joins the user to a Facebook group named "SNS—Social Network Suiciders." Simultaneously, it starts to remove connections to Facebook friends one by one. The whole process is automated and visible to the user. His Facebook life is disappearing in front of the user's eyes. Also, *Web 2.0 Suicide Machine* has a ranking system in which the more friends a user gets to join him before the suicide, the more highly the user is ranked.

Seppukoo.com and *Web 2.0 Suicide Machine* demonstrate quite clearly how tactical media emerge with their target. As Raley has stated, "tactical media comes so close to its core informational and technological apparatuses that protest in a sense becomes the mirror image of its object, its aesthetic replicatory and reiterative rather than strictly oppositional."[76] Both digital suicide services use Facebook's own logic to function and spread. If the aim of Facebook is to envelop the user's life inside the network, *Seppukoo.com* and *Web 2.0 Suicide Machine* do the inverse by affirming and embracing death.

Consequently, *Seppukoo.com*'s and *Web 2.0 Suicide Machine*'s connections to the Facebook environment also entail their connection to Facebook's biopolitical business model, which is phrased as a question in Dockray's "Facebook Suicide Bomb Manifesto": "When someone disappears from Facebook, does anyone notice?"[77] The answer, of course, is yes. The suicide of the user is updated in his Facebook status; the user is added to the group of social network suiciders; even the profile picture is changed to remind others of the digital death of the user. On one hand *Seppukoo.com* and *Web 2.0 Suicide Machine* are not detached or freed from the business logic: everything becomes a post that can be clicked and liked. On the other, however, digital suicide is a way to affirm different life. *Seppukoo.com* and *Web 2.0 Suicide Machine* control and guide users in selecting another way of life disconnected from the premediated workings of Facebook but nevertheless connected to the potentials and possibilities the service provides. For there would be no digital suicide without Facebook, and without Facebook's impressive machinery of attention economy, no one would know about it. As Dockray puts it, "social networks need a social suicide."[78]

Digital Suicide: Data

In addition to social suicide, another side of digital suicide should be accounted for. Dockray's manifesto articulates this side as a question concerning social media data mining: "Does this software retroactively invalidate all of the marketing data that has been collected from the account?"[79] The artworks discussed in this chapter do not answer to the question, but they do indicate a potential for resistance. To begin with, let us follow Raley, who, paraphrasing Foucault, points out that there is no single locus of refusal but a plurality of resistances in tactical media.[80] Instead of replacing one ideology with another, tactical media supplement their targets with creative destruction.[81] If we consider digital suicide as creative destruction, it seems evident that it is something more than simply a termination of one's user account. In fact, death, as Deleuze notes, always seems to be a double. On one hand, there is the very personal death of the individual, the I who dies; on the other, there is the impersonal death, the one who dies, which refers to the virtual power of endlessly becoming other outside the forms and mold of the I or ego.[82]

This double nature of death surrounds digital suicide. It leaves a data trace that can be followed. When an individual is using *Seppukoo.com* or *Web 2.0 Suicide Machine* to access her Facebook account, her online identity is given to software and its automated processes. When the password and user name are set, the suicide begins. In consequence, the offline individual is cut off from her Facebook profile. A reference point here is the concept of the dividual and its death. It is at this very moment when the online identity loses its attachments to the molding I of the offline identity. Thus the question is not what happens to the offline individual who is now cut off from Facebook but, on the contrary, what happens to the online identity. The online identity is key to understanding how digital suicide exceeds, for example, Shannon's machine's biased models of being either "on" or "off" and affirms the double nature of dying as creative destruction. It is the impersonal dimension of death we are interested in—*Seppukoo.com*'s invitation to "rediscover the importance of being anyone, instead of pretending to be someone."[83]

The goal of *Seppukoo.com* and *Web 2.0 Suicide Machine* is to break the representational scheme between the online identity and the offline individual. Thus the goal is not simply to help the users quit but to introduce different potential ways to exist in social networks. We can follow a similar train of thought in Briz's work. Here, rather than putting brackets on the latter part of the title of his work, *How to/Why Leave Facebook (on My Own Terms, without "Deleting" My Account),* one should highlight it, for it guides us to a fundamental split in one's online identity, where one side is formed by individual interactions and the other is conditioned by the platform. Briz shows that there are alternatives to deleting one's account without removing it from the platform entirely. In his artwork, Briz gives detailed instructions how users can delete all Facebook activity, photos, tags, and Wall posts; the instructions also include how to leave groups and unfriend all friends. For the removal of some of these features, Briz has developed a code, which, for example, in the context of unfriending, will take over control of the user's mouse and unfriend all her friends on behalf of the individual. After the removal, what is left is a vacated Facebook profile that no longer has any active or visible relations to other users, things, and surroundings. Briz's approach to leaving on one's own terms is to create a unique manifestation of online identity, which is given a nonexistence that is full in the sense that it does not refer to any other subject than itself.

Arguably, an identity like this, which remains on Facebook after digital suicide but does not participate, becomes meaningless for the machinic subjectivation of capitalism: it does not produce new data for marketing. It is not representative for statistical analysis because it does not represent an individual or a population who exists. Simultaneously, its actions cannot be anticipated and premediated because it does not have any. It remains in the network as passive and ascetic. In this sense, it is nonexistent and becomes absolutely irrelevant to controlling authorities.[84]

The *Web 2.0 Suicide Machine* does the same thing as Briz but takes the performance to the next level by generating a Facebook group of "SNS—Social Network Suiciders."[85] This group is a population of online identities cut off from their offline individuals. This group forms a mass of the "generalized dynamics" that emerge when someone extracts "attributes, predicates, qualities or references from a large group of people."[86] Users' private information, such as email notifications, friends, groups, and Wall posts, are removed. One ceases to be social. One's data turn meaningless. The part of the dividual that remains on Facebook has no worth for targeted marketing. It remains in the network not as an individual but as part of a multitude of others who have also committed virtual suicide. Machinic subjectivities are turned into machinic collectivities.

Interestingly, digital suicide begins to appear as a passive rather than an active form of resistance. If we turn to the online identity disconnected from the Facebook user, it reminds us of the death of Bartleby the Scrivener in Herman Melville's short story, whose refusal "I would prefer not to" resulted in the end in isolation from the surrounding environment and death by starvation.[87] Quite similarly, through digital suicide, the user cedes power to Facebook but retains the power to withhold. The identity stays on Facebook but does not fit into its user representations or biopolitical models of data mining. The remnant does not affirm or negate anything particular on Facebook. It is an identity without reference or preferences.[88]

As an affirmation of Michael Hardt and Antonio Negri's demand that it takes a network to fight a network; the group of social network suiciders aggregates these remnants without particularities.[89] It is a machinic collectivity that works against data mining with its own logic. It creates a multitude of passive nodes whose data are meaningless and cannot be exploited via commercial means. It is a multitude of virtual suiciders whose identities remain and continue their own lives without the other half of the dividual. They do not actively participate in Facebook's normal activities, such as writing Wall posts, creating status updates, updating photos, or commenting on others' posts. Indeed, these remnants of suicide become what Mejias has described as paranodes.[90] They are nodes that do not conform to the logics of the network but instead occupy the space between active nodes and their links. Yet they are involved in the topological act of linking by being collapsed, bypassed, or bumped into.

"Don't become nothing, the singular point defined by an absence, become everything, with everyone else," the "Facebook Suicide Bomb Manifesto" calls, and as we have seen, this is indeed just what Briz's work and also *Seppukoo.com* and *Web 2.0 Suicide Machine* aim to do.[91] Committing digital suicide with these services does not mean disappearing from the networks or nonbeing in them. Instead, it denotes the virtual side of reality, the creative potentiality to become something other outside actualized forms of being.[92] After digital suicide, masses have ceased to be a subject and cannot be given a subject position. Indeed, the masses of suiciders are what really disturb the biopolitical business logic of social media: passive identities who do not like any pages, do not share any information, do not allow their identities to become products for consuming. They just remain on Facebook, altering its development and also reminding others that there are methods of disconnecting oneself.

Die

For the sake of argument, consider yourself at the moment of your own death. A few hours after the rumors about your death have become public knowledge, people seek to confirm the information from your Facebook profile. The more famous you are, the more quickly the rumor spreads. Updating your own Facebook status is impossible, because you are dead. Without the chance to intervene, your Facebook News Feed begins to fill up with condolences from your friends and acquaintances, or it might even be targeted by RIP trolls posting nasty comments and making fun of your final departure. If you have been a perspicacious user and aged nineteen or older, you have prepared for the situation by assigning a Legacy Contact. Since 2015, Facebook has allowed users to choose a Facebook friend who would take over the Facebook account in the event of the death of the account holder. The Legacy Contact can, for example, add a pinned post to share a final message, respond to new friend requests, change the cover and profile photo, or request that the account be deleted. The Legacy Contact cannot, however, remove friends or accept new friends, read messages, or delete or alter past posts on your behalf. In fact, and for the platform to govern the uses of the accounts of the dead, the Legacy Contact will not get access to one's Facebook profile as such, but the account needs to be memorialized first.[1]

"Facebook serves as a graveyard for an estimated 50 million people, with three million more Facebook users—at the very least—dying every year," George Harrison writes for the *Sun* newspaper.[2] In 2098, according to other statistics, the number of dead users on Facebook will outnumber the living.[3] "Facebook's design and management teams have a huge ongoing task to create, maintain, and adapt software controls to deal with an enormous and ever-growing 'dead' population among a wider social network of living 'friends,'" Bjorn Nansen with his colleagues argue.[4] By investigating the inauguration of Facebook's policies on death and different practices surrounding dead Facebook users—of which a memorialized account is one example—I outline an understanding of how life and death are embedded within social media platforms. When life and death become entangled with media technology, they also become subjects and objects of certain particular forms of politics. In this context, two specific models of politics that operate behind the Facebook platform are important: biopolitics and noopolitics. These are politics that address the economic, biological, and spiritual lives of a population and politics that address ways of living, feeling, thinking, and acting through mediated technologies.[5] Moreover, to specify these politics, I follow Bruno Latour and Vincent Lépinay's argument that "*economics and politics deal with the same object,* follow the same fabric, feel their way around the same networks, depend on the same influences and the same contaminations."[6] This approach continues my pursuits to draw attention to the social media platform itself and to build an understanding of how, through disconnection, the user participation paradigm, with its inscribed ideas of user activity, becomes challenged. With this shift, I do not want to downplay the meaningfulness of Facebook for grievers; rather, I want to show in a more abstract manner how death and the dead find their place within media technologies that have become ubiquitous and permeate all aspects of our lives. As I show in this chapter, life, as well as death, is built into these platforms in a very concrete sense.

Ground

The question of life ending and the consecutive processes of grieving and mourning will "increasingly become important aspects of our social experiences online."[7] Indeed, as Nancy Baym argues, "since 2008, SNS [social network sites] have become mainstream sites of relational maintenance for those who already know one another."[8] The relations we have with other users, our Facebook friends, for example, are personally felt and experienced. Social media empower users to build

personal connections, generate content, and participate in various social activities together. Similarly, when one of your friends breathes her
last breath, Facebook is the obvious place where these intimate and
private relations are also shared and commemorated.

These novel experiences of death and dying are also increasingly
being studied. Many studies focus on the particular rituals and processes of online grieving. Jed Brubaker and Gillian Hayes have explained how personal and cultural practices of experiencing death are
entwined with communicational practices of social media platforms.[9]
Rebecca Kern, Abbe Forman, and Gisela Gil-Equi have argued that
Facebook enables new, public ways to process grieving.[10] Alice Marwick and Nicole B. Ellison have focused on performative displays of
grieving and argued that bereavement in Facebook can be discussed as
the impression management of the deceased.[11]

Whereas death is an individual event, the processes of mourning
online are collective and social. There are different audiences for the
dead, different ways to engage with the dead, and different relations
that need not be personal. Marwick and Ellison, for example, note
that

> the quasi-public nature of social media means that information
> about the death will also be shared with a larger public. . . . These
> audiences may include strangers who wish to take part in expres-
> sions of public mourning (sometimes dismissively called "grief
> tourists") or "trolls" (people who post deliberately inflammatory
> messages with a disruptive intent, usually under a pseudonym).[12]

The dead online touch upon different users and become the basis for
different modes of participation. In short, studies focusing on online
grieving share a user-centric approach. The role of the deceased is,
however, subordinate to the different modes of user participation and
cultural expression performed by the bereaved, grief tourists, and
other agents instead.

The user-centric approach focusing on events and expressions taking place among the bereaved corresponds to the discourses of Web
2.0 platforms and the emphasized role of the user as cultural producer and the consequent harnessing of these users into productive
processes. To put it bluntly, users contribute to these productive processes in two different ways: the first way is intentional and explicit,

and the second is unintentional and implicit.[13] To begin with, the former user participation is commonly paralleled with the concept of user-generated content. According to Andreas Kaplan and Michael Haenlein, user-generated content describes "various forms of media content that is publicly available and created by end-users."[14] Defining the concept further, they argue that user-generated content needs to be publicly available, show an amount of creative effort, and be made by amateurs. This explicit participation is based on users' own processes of creating, sharing, and participating in various activities on the site. The latter describes participation in Web 2.0 platforms in another manner. It is a form of participation where users produce information for the site through their activities implicitly, and often without knowing. As Mark Andrejevic maintains, the ideal of user-generated content as participatory amateur media production is contrasted and conjoined with user-generated content that "includes the tremendous amounts of data that consumers generate about themselves when they interact with a new generation of networked digital devices."[15] Social media companies profit from these implicit actions by transforming user data into clusters of information offered to third parties or used by the company itself. Hence user participation, understood as activities producing user-generated content, is double-sided; it consists of the content generated by the users themselves and the content generated from users by the platform.

The dead user pushes us to reconsider the ideas of user participation and user-generated content as core features of social media from another angle; the dead are not active content producers or data generators by themselves. They neither produce content nor provide activities, consumption habits, or other information for the platform to track and monitor. For the participatory web and the corresponding Web 2.0 business models, the dead are nothing more than waste. They do not actively participate or couple with media technologies. They do not interact or give feedback. The dead cease to be with us as physical and corporeal beings but also as interactive actors in network environments. It would seem that they are futile for social media platforms. Consequently, it seems legitimate to subordinate dead users to processes of online grieving and explain this as a social event and a particular mode of user participation evolving around the deceased.

Yet, I want to highlight the role of the dead for the platform.

Arguably, the dead are indeed futile, but only until the very moment they are incorporated by Facebook through different policies and technical implementations, such as memorial pages and memorial profiles. When the dead are materialized to the site through memorialization, they are also utilized and given a specific role.

To better understand the role of the dead user for Facebook as well as processes of online grieving, one must take a step backward from the user-centric approach. The role of the Facebook platform and its policies on the dead can be approached directly, instead of trying to find the answers from personal processes of online grieving. Consequently, my focus in the remainder of this article is not on the communicational processes in which the grievers take part but on looking at what happens to the dead themselves and how they become a part of the platform.

This, then, is a study of the platform rather than a study of the user, whether dead or alive, and it emphasizes the active and generative role of the platform in social media relationships. Therefore, in the definition of a platform, I am following Tarleton Gillespie, who argues that the choices of a given platform "about what can appear, how it is organized, how it is monetized, what can be removed and why, and what the technical architecture allows and prohibits, are all real and substantive interventions into the contours of public discourse."[16] What should be noted, however, is that the user-centric approaches, while focusing on users' reactions and experiences, touch upon the role of the platform in dealing with the online dead. For Marwick and Ellison, the platform is a technological and social platform that guides users' behaviors and outlines the "technical and social affordances."[17] Similarly, Brubaker and Hayes analyze how technologically mediated communication practices guide the ways we interact with the dead and each other.[18] Indeed, these discussions also point out that there are platform-specific ways to deal with death; they indicate that there are Facebook-specific ways of processing and managing the dead online.

Biopolitics or Hiding Dead Bodies

"Each death is unique, of course, and therefore unusual, but what can one say about the unusual when . . . it multiplies . . . as in series?" Jacques Derrida asks.[19] In recent years, social media have been faced with this question.[20] The answers have been outlined in various forms, from blog posts to official policies and guidelines. Here I focus on research materials that explain the inauguration of Facebook's policies regarding dead users[21] and the concurrent Facebook guidelines for what users could do to dead user profiles after the policy changes.[22]

On the *Facebook Blog,* Facebook's chief security officer, Max Kelly, describes the personal event, the death of a coworker, that led to the inauguration of Facebook's current policies regarding the dead:

> About six weeks after we both started [working for Facebook], my best friend was killed in a tragic bicycling accident. It was a big blow to me personally, but it also was difficult for everyone at Facebook. We were a small, tight-knit community, and any single tragedy had a great effect on all of us. I can recall a company-wide meeting a few days after his death, where I spoke about what my friend meant to me and what we had hoped to do together. As a company, we shared our grief, and for many people it was their first interaction with death. . . . The question soon came up: What do we do about his Facebook profile? We had never really thought about this before in such a personal way. Obviously, we wanted to be able to model people's relationships on Facebook, but how do you deal with an interaction with someone who is no longer able to log on? When someone leaves us, they don't leave our memories or our social network.[23]

On one hand, the motivations for inauguration of Facebook's policies regarding dead users are personal and originate with a tragic emotional experience. On the other hand, they are platform political responses to the growing number of dead users and driven by a motivation to implement life with its entirety within the Facebook platform.

Indeed, for me, the discussions of death and the dead in social media are connected to the discussions that try to understand how life takes place and finds new forms in our current media landscape. "Media determine our situation," as Friedrich Kittler puts it.[24] Media rewire our senses, and it is through media technologies that we think, act, and feel. Our daily lives are so connected to media technologies that it is difficult to distinguish between the human and the technological. Kittler challenges the idea of the human actor and the centrality of human life as lived experience in media environments as such. As Geoffrey

Winthrop-Young explains, for Kittler, "humans are at best along for the ride; more precisely, they are the nodes and operators necessary to keep the process going until the time arrives at which media are able to interact and evolve without any human go-between."[25] While Kittler's view may be extreme, the idea of media technologies being a part of the mundane activities of a user's daily life has recently become commonplace. This is broadly evident in the discourses of computers becoming ubiquitous and of life shared and lived in social media but also in ideals like peer production. Life and media permeate each other in many ways.

The problematic role of media life, of humans existing with or in media, is indicative of how the issue is also political. Michel Foucault's lectures of the 1970s have long since inaugurated a revitalized discussion about the relationship between life and politics through the concept of biopolitics.[26] Biopolitics for Foucault, in essence, is a system of power where life becomes regulated and controlled through governmental actions. The right to take life is bound up with the power to make live and let die. The life of the individual is contrasted with a more general understanding of the life of a population. Fertility and morbidity enter into the biopolitical after birth control and self-care are introduced. And I here wish to draw attention to how these governmental actions are coupled with what Maurizio Lazzarato defines as "technologies of the social"[27] that, as Tiziana Terranova suggests, "do not aim to suspend the 'interplay of reality' that supposedly belongs to the domain of nature, but are determined to act within it."[28] In effect, when life becomes politicized, it also becomes embedded within a battery of different technologies of which social media platforms are one. As conjoined with ubiquitous technologies, biopolitics does not mean enslaving new media users, nor does it introduce a conspiracy theory of an outside control. Instead, as John Cheney-Lippold notes, it introduces a model of soft control in the lives of users; new media technologies, for example, provide a set of possible identities and offer a set of possible actions users can do.[29]

Now, if life is the focus of these new technologies, what should we think about death? The relation of biopolitics and death has always been problematic. With an emphasis on making life live, biopolitics pushes death into the shadows. According to Foucault, death and dying lose their roles as rituals and spectacles and become a problem for society, because they decrease growth and work efficiency; when the life of a population becomes the focus, death as an individual event essentially becomes private and hidden away.[30]

To understand why the dead are problematic for Facebook and why they are a matter of biopolitics, one must begin from the fact that dying does not erase the user's account automatically. Quite the contrary: the user's account remains on the site. The user accounts of the dead are a constant reminder of the deceased and the fragility of life lived outside social media, but they are also a technical problem. To substantiate this point, let me refer to Kelly's blog post regarding the inauguration of Facebook's policies on the dead.[31] Interestingly, Kelly points out that Facebook's policies on the dead appeared only a week after a new feature was introduced that suggested users reconnect with friends with whom they had not been in contact lately. These suggestions were presumably controlled with algorithms that could not tell the difference between the dead and the living user. As Whitney Phillips notes, this feature was quickly proven problematic, because "the dead person's profile would occasionally show up in friends' suggestion boxes ('Reconnect with Bill by posting something on his wall!'), prompting a number of users to complain."[32] Although this new feature was a constant reminder of the deceased and caused resentment, it also revealed that Facebook was developing new ways to manage its users.

As a response to this problem, Facebook created two possible solutions: *removing the account* and *memorializing the account*. To begin with the former, when the user is no longer able to log on owing to her death, the power to control the user account is given to friends and the family:

> Verified immediate family members may request the removal of a
> loved one's account from the site. We will process certain special
> requests for verified immediate family members, including requests
> to remove a loved one's account. This will completely remove the
> profile (timeline) and all associated content from Facebook, so no
> one can view it.[33]

After removal of the account, the user disappears from Facebook. Their profile page cannot be found or accessed. Removing the deceased user account seems to corroborate the biopolitical understanding of social media. When life lived on Facebook is semipublic at the very least, because your friends see what you do and how you participate, death will be pushed into the shadows and made a private event. The deceased becomes hidden from the platform.

Now, removing the Facebook user account of a deceased member is possible, but it is not particularly easy. According to the Facebook Help Center, family of the deceased can remove the Facebook account of the dead if the requester has relevant certificates proving a relationship with the user and proof of her death. Quoting these instructions at length is necessary here to explicate the process:

> For all special requests, we require verification that you are an immediate family member or executor. Requests will not be processed if we are unable to verify your relationship to the deceased.
>
> Examples of documentation that we will accept include:
>
> The deceased's birth certificate
>
> The deceased's death certificate
>
> Proof of authority under local law that you are the lawful representative of the deceased or his/her estate.[34]

If the dead are what Facebook hides, why is deleting the account so difficult? Is the demand to provide official documents and certificates merely a question of privacy and an attempt to secure that no accounts can be removed accidentally or maliciously? The difficulty of deleting Facebook user accounts needs to take into account another consideration. In fact, the difficulty of deleting dead user profiles may well imply that Facebook does not want the dead user accounts to be removed at all. Thus, as a second response to the problem of dead users, Facebook suggests a process of memorialization. It is a response that not only hides the dead but also gives them a new role. Specifically, the dead as well as the processes of mourning become governed through platform applications known as memorialized user accounts.

Memorializing accounts instead of removing them is relatively simple.[35] To memorialize a user account, one does not have to provide legal documentation, such as a birth or death certificate, for the user. To memorialize an account, one need only fill out a Memorializing Request Form, where the user needs to explain his relation to the deceased and present proof of the death, which can be an obituary or news article, for example.[36]

Memorialized accounts are Facebook's unique manifestation of the dead within the platform. According to Kelly, Facebook "created the idea of 'memorialized' profiles as a place where people can save and share their memories of those who've passed."[37] Phillips calls these memorialized accounts a snapshot of the user's life just before her death.[38] In brief, a memorialized account is the person's own user account converted into a memorial state. As Facebook explains, this memorial state means, for example, that some of the functions associated with normal user accounts are limited:

> When someone passes away, Facebook will memorialize their account in order to protect their privacy. Memorialization changes the account's privacy settings so that only confirmed friends can see that person's profile or find them by typing their name into the search bar. A memorialized account will also be removed from the Suggestions section of the Home Page, and no birthday reminders will be sent out on their behalf. To further protect the account, no one is allowed to log in or receive login information about it. One important change Facebook has recently made to this process is that when we memorialize an account, we now preserve past Wall posts, so that friends and family can look back on memories of the loved one they lost. We also now allow confirmed Facebook friends to continue posting on the memorialized account's Wall. They can record memories, leave condolences, and provide information about funeral services.[39]

Memorializing a user account hides the dead, quite literally, from the public Facebook search and from people with whom the deceased is not connected. It does not, however, erase the person or his memory. The dead remain on the platform currently with the word "Remembering" showing "next to the person's name on their profile."[40] Thus memorialized accounts are a way to organize, classify, and define bodies into particular categories. Memorialized accounts do not pop up in searches or mix the operations of different algorithms. Memorialized accounts are Facebook's way of differentiating the dead and the living.

If death is, as Foucault maintains, the moment "when the individual escapes all power, falls back on himself and retreats, so to speak, into his own privacy,"[41] Facebook not only protects this privacy through memorialized accounts but turns it into a new mode of interaction. "While there is no cure for the pain of grief, Facebook's hope is that by allowing people to mourn together, the grieving process will be alleviated just a little bit."[42] Memorialized accounts enable new modes of collaboration, participation, and production with the dead. After the user account is memorialized, the privacy into which the deceased retreats becomes controlled by the platform. The escaping of all power is temporary, because after the death, this power is not handed to the user or her friends and family but to the social media platform, which now preserves the account.

Noopolitics, or the Memories of the Deceased

While the discussions around online grieving circulate around how people use social media platforms for purposes of processing a personal loss, Facebook's policies on dead users require us to consider how the dead users are themselves used by the platform. To elaborate further on the meaning of memorial accounts, I follow Lazzarato's suggestion that biopolitics needs to be supplemented with noopolitics.[43] This means moving from the technologies governing the body toward technologies that gather publics together and control their actions.

Before moving on to the theme of noopolitics, one should note that Facebook practices two different forms of memorializing deceased users. A memorialized user account, as discussed earlier, is a user's personal account converted into a memorial state. A memorial page, on the other hand, is a page established by other people, for example, loved ones or friends.[44] From a biopolitical perspective, memorialized accounts differ from memorial pages because they are Facebook's way of distinguishing between the user accounts of the dead and those of the living. However, both page types revolve around the deceased by gathering users and working as platforms for grieving. This practice of convening a group of people to share memories and thoughts connects memorial pages and memorialized user accounts to noopolitics. In noopolitics, the question is no longer so much about regulating individuals and manipulating individual bodies as it is about controlling mass behavior and building collective intelligence. Noopolitics denotes ways of steering heterogeneous groups and publics from a distance through, for example, media technologies that affect mind, memory, and attention.[45] Commenting on noopolitics, Tiziana Terranova notes that

> a public . . . is always the result of a certain kind of affective capture (a public can be generated by a film, a TV serial, a book, a speaker, a news event, an artwork, a cultural initiative, a blog), which can be one-directional but also reciprocal (it is not just that publics are the provisional result of a capture, but they can also capture and take control of novels, TV serials, radio programmes, blogs, speakers, etc.).[46]

Noopolitics does not describe novel mechanisms of power, nor does it propose that users or media audiences are brainwashed as such. Instead, it tries to explicate how these publics are formed and how they operate under the noopolitical regime.

Memorialized accounts are a perfect example of the affective capture Terranova describes. By memorializing dead users' accounts, Facebook aims to offer a platform where "people who use [our] service [have] a chance to mourn together and remember someone who passed away, people can find comfort in sharing happy and heartwarming stories about their departed friend or family member."[47] Memorialized accounts can been seen as a technique to "translate disconnection into new connections";[48] the deceased is the uniting cause that brings the public together. The memorialized account or the memorial page is the place where "the 'friends' collectively remember the deceased, engaging in ritualistic behaviors akin to behaviors performed at wakes, burials, and cemetery visits."[49] They are built through "*sharing memories* of the deceased, *posting updates* from their own lives, and leaving comments that evidence a desire for *maintaining connections* with the deceased."[50]

However, we should not take memorial accounts or memorial pages merely as places for users to gather and mourn together. Instead, I propose that they should be interpreted as agencies that have the capability to affect how users act, think, and behave. Online grieving is not only a social and personal experience but also an experience guided and controlled by platform-specific functions. This kind of approach to memorial sites corresponds to Robert W. Gehl's argument that, when interpreted through noopolitics, Facebook's core functions, such as the Like button and recommendation features, can be seen as structuring the way we think in and with social media.[51] For the remainder of this chapter, I turn to how memorial pages and memorialized accounts gather people together and, in doing so, structure the way the deceased are perceived, understood, and remembered.

To begin with, consider a Facebook remembrance project organized by the Belgian National Institute for Veterans and Victims of War called Live and Remember.[52] The idea for the Live and Remember project is simple: people are asked to choose to tell a story of an Allied soldier of the Second World War with a memorial page on Facebook. First, the user is asked to pick a soldier from the 25,360 Allied soldiers buried in Belgium. Then, the user starts mining relevant data regarding the selected soldier. The story of the soldier is elaborated on the memorial page through pictures, maps, and videos—by the means common to Facebook activity. Through the data on this individual soldier, a memory is activated and his life story is brought to attention.

Important for the argument I am developing here is that the Facebook memorial account, the dead user profile, need not be interpreted according to the similarities between the offline and online user or the life he lived. The user profile, the Timeline and its memories, and different relations among users can be fabricated. This concerns both the memorialized user account and the memorial page. As Marwick and Ellison point out, these page types do not solely represent the life of the user.[53] They are not only storage places for the life lived (past events, meaningful moments) but also places where new impressions of the deceased are created and shared. Because the deceased is not present to censor or monitor what is said about him, impression management is in the hands of other users.[54] Thus what is essential for these pages is the capability, not to guide the pages' viewers in remembering the deceased, but rather a more abstract modulation of memory that is built through what is clicked and which recommendations are followed.

This modulation of memory and its harnessing into creating new things is one of the most important functions of noopolitics. Lazzarato, referring to Henri Bergson's reversed cone in *Matter and Memory*, explains how remembering is not a reproduction of the past but its creation and individuation.[55] For something new to emerge, there always needs to be a memory. Paraphrasing Lazzarato, if there were no memory, no force of duration that preserves the past in the present, the world would start endlessly: "any sensation developing itself over time, requires a force which conserves that which is no more within that which is; a duration which conserves the dead in the alive."[56] Memorial pages and memorialized accounts conserve the dead in the living in a very literal sense. A posted picture of the deceased, a comment on the Wall, and other acts of mourning create new connections, new ideas; in other words, they actualize the virtual.

This view helps us understand the political implications behind Facebook's policy of memorializing all user accounts instead of deleting them. When converted to memorial accounts and memorial pages, the dead are given a certain agency. They become points where memories are activated and, in some cases, fabricated. As platforms for online grieving, these pages allow the dead to become nodes that open up toward other nodes and other agencies. Memorial pages and memorialized user accounts specifically corroborate a notion of Latour et al. that, since the introduction of user profiles, individuals have become temporary passing points defined not by themselves but by networks of connections with which they are associated.[57] Such profiles can be called *monads*. A "monad is not a part of a whole, but a *point of view* on all the other entities taken *severally* and not as a totality."[58] A practical example of a monad is a person searched for on the web. At first, the person is nothing but a name or a clickable entity. Then, through search results, we slowly begin to fill in more and more items of the person's profile. The list of elements with which the person is associated will eventually specify her. According to Latour et al., the "point of this navigation is that it does not *start* with substitutable individuals . . . but *individualizes* an entity by deploying its attributes."[59]

Thus the politics of memorial pages and memorialized user accounts are not merely the politics of representing individuals. On the contrary, an individual is only a small part of this assemblage of data and activation of memory through which Facebook and social media platforms remain operational. Consider again the Live and Remember project. While the soldier whose memorial page is created becomes individualized through the network of relations, the event of World War II is simultaneously folded within that same network. World War II is seen through this individual. The individual is a navigational spot with a potentiality to open a perspective on the world from a certain political perspective. In the case of Live and Remember, this is the Allied perspective and a Western perspective. But it is also a Facebook-specific perspective operating through the functions the platform enables and allows. As Latour et al. describe, "it begins as a dot, a spot, and it ends (provisionally) as a monad with an interior encapsulated into an envelope. Were the inquiry to continue, the 'whole world,' as Leibniz said, would be 'grasped' or 'reflected' through this idiosyncratic point of view."[60] Consequently, memorial pages and online grieving are never only personal experiences or related to the deceased. Quite the contrary, they are enfolded within the surrounding world.

If we follow Latour and Lépinay's suggestion that politics and economics weave the same networks,[61] it is possible to show that memorialized user accounts and memorial pages are Facebook's way of utilizing the dead and granting them agency. This conversion of dead user profiles into memorial accounts "thingifies" the deceased, and when user profiles become things, they have not only personal or cultural value but also use-value and exchange-value.[62] The dead become a new ground for user participation. Memorialized accounts and memorial pages are able to generate affective relationships from beyond the grave by grouping people together, giving things to be shared and thought of together. Although the dead themselves do not participate in actions, share things, or directly contribute to the accumulation of user information, they yet become navigational points for other users' participation. When user accounts become memorialized, quoting Scott Lash and Celia Lury, "we enter a world of operationality, a world not of interpretation but of navigation."[63] Then, the interest, for the platform, is no longer how we remember the deceased but what we do to them or do with them online; what kind of data can be accumulated through these actions, and what kind of preferences do they reveal? As Tama Leaver puts it, "for Facebook, while posthumous users do not generate data themselves, the fact that they were part of a network means that their connections may interact with a memorialised account, or memorial page, and this activity, like all Facebook activities, allows the platform to display advertising and further track user interactions."[64] Facebook's policies on death and different practices surrounding the dead Facebook user are not done only for the sake of an individual but also for the sake of the networks and connections the individual potentially holds.

Disconnect

After some reflection, I've decided to delete my account on
Facebook. I'd like to encourage you to do the same. This is part
altruism and part selfish. The altruism part is that I think Facebook, as a company, is unethical. The selfish part is that I'd like my
own social network to migrate away from Facebook so that I'm
not missing anything.[1]

In this short passage, Dan Yoder explains his solution to leave Facebook on the Gizmodo technology blog in 2010 and encourages other
users to follow his lead. Yoder's proclamation points toward two
problems Facebook criticism has addressed throughout the existence
of the platform. The first is ethical: social media are seen to have the
potential to compromise our privacy by, for example, mining and exploiting the personal data we submit on the platform. The second is
social: there is a concern that the more our private lives and social
relationships become intertwined with social media, the harder it is to
leave. Social media captures social relations too well. What is shared
with both problems is the idea that on social media, we are never connected only with our "friends" and "followers" but we also bond with
the platform that guides and maintains our relationships. The solution
to disconnect, as Yoder points out, is also inadequate if it does not
become social and attract other users as well.

Gilles Deleuze and Félix Guattari argue that all "concepts are connected to problems without which they would have no meaning and
which can themselves only be isolated or understood as their solution

emerges."[2] Starting from Yoder's example, this chapter aims to show how disconnection as a conceptual framework lets us understand different problems and solutions of our culture of connectivity. The dictionary definition of the noun *disconnect* as (1) an "instance of disconnecting or being disconnected" or (2) a "discrepancy or lack of connection" indicates already that there are different kinds of problems and solutions.[3] To return to Yoder's example, the first definition points toward the social issues and the second toward the ethical issues of social media connectivity. What I will demonstrate through various different examples of the events where disconnection appears is that neither solutions nor problems can be reduced to simple binaries where, for example, logging in would give users the capacity to act and logging out would remove this capacity, or vice versa. As the discussion in the previous chapter illustrates, even the moment of death does not disconnect us from our Facebook accounts; we need to assign a proxy to pull that plug. Even in the moment of death, social media are "connective media."[4] Here again, both sides of the noun *disconnect* are present, in the form of power relations, if nothing else. In the following, I draw a map to the cultures of disconnectivity consisting of traces of events, responses, manifestations, accidents, and breaks that are scattered across the field of social media. The culture of disconnectivity is of variations, differences, and repetitions of particular human acts, such as leaving, diaspora, and death, but it is also about the politics of the platform and the attempts to maintain and manage the bonds it constantly creates and renews. To examine disconnection is to show that on social media platforms, the questions of agency are complicated, nuanced, and related to myriad connections between social, technological, political, and economic factors.

Alternatives

On May 31, 2010, a group of dissatisfied Facebook users organized a Quit Facebook Day. The idea was that during that particular day, users would mass protest against Facebook by leaving the site. More specifically, the protesters were protesting against Facebook's data policies and against the platform not giving the users enough freedom of choice or control related to what happens to their information. Quit Facebook Day, however, was not a tremendous success. Out of

450 million Facebook users, only thirty-one thousand users decided to disconnect that day. This was hardly a surprise for the organizers, who declared:

> Quitting Facebook isn't easy. Facebook is engaging, enjoyable and quite frankly, addictive. Quitting something like Facebook is like quitting smoking. It's hard to stay on the wagon long enough to actually change your habits. Having peer support helps, but the way to quit Facebook is not to start a group on Facebook about leaving Facebook.[5]

Although Quit Facebook Day failed, its different cultural tropes have remained until today. First is the idea that Facebook is addictive like a drug. Second is the idea that there could be social media alternatives that would be more fair and open, or at least different. For example, in 2011, the developers of Facebook alternative Diaspora* stated that they were building "a new and better social web, one that's 100% owned and controlled by you and other Diasporans." The platform's name "Diaspora*" references the dispersion of a people from their original homeland, and while not naming its enemy, Diaspora* states that it was developed against the control of big corporations and founded on the ideas of decentralization, anonymity, real connections, and social freedom. Reading between the lines, we can see a targeted criticism toward Facebook and other commercialized social media sites. In particular, Diaspora* is designed to allow people to disconnect from social media sites that allegedly ascribe to a business logic that exploits users and their information.[6]

These discourses seem typical for Facebook alternatives. Another example is Ello, which gained public attention in 2014 when Facebook threatened to suspend the accounts of known drag queens who were, against Facebook's real-name policy, using the platform with their chosen names.[7] Ello became a platform to which users who wanted to appear with their chosen names started to migrate. Ello does not promise user anonymity as such, but it does promise a platform that is "not a tool to deceive, coerce and manipulate—but a place to connect, create and celebrate life."[8] Similar to Diaspora*, Ello is also positioned against social media data mining and selling this user information for advertisers. Ello's website declares that it is an alternative for the current social media sites you are using, which are "owned by advertisers" and "every post you share, every friend you make and every link you follow is tracked, recorded and converted into data. Advertisers buy your data so they can show you more ads. You are the product that's bought and sold."[9]

These social media alternatives argue that to find alternatives to the current business logic of social media sites, we need to disconnect from the old ones. But what in fact is this logic, and where did it come from? As we know, for the past decade, social media have been about enabling, establishing, and exploiting connections between people, communities, markets, participation, ideas, and other actors. Our current model of online connectivity can be traced back to the burst of the dot-com bubble in 2001. The dot-com bubble was caused by the expansion of web-related businesses, which aimed at growing their user bases even if doing so produced substantial annual losses. "Get big fast" was the main business ideology. At the height of the boom, these companies entered stock markets without revenue or profit. Soon the economy crashed, and many of these companies folded.

In the dot-com bubble, new online connectivity had led into an economic collapse. Merely the number of users did not guarantee economic success for these new companies. However, some of the companies had survived. In what I would call one of the first studies of online disconnection, Tim O'Reilly coined the concept of Web 2.0 by analyzing big web businesses that had survived the dot-com crash. What he found was that the survivors had not only gathered a large user base but also "embraced the power of the web to harness collective intelligence."[10] O'Reilly describes how successful online businesses not only provide a platform for user participation but, to put it bluntly, also exploit this participation. Specifically, O'Reilly talks about Amazon, Google, and Wikipedia. Amazon survived the dot-com crash by redefining the web bookstore business by implementing user participation within its interface. Amazon enables users to produce content, such as book reviews, but it also exploits users by monitoring their activity and transforming it into better search results. Google enables users to search information, and with the PageRank algorithm, it exploits this information to manage and provide targeted search results. In addition, activities such as updating Wikipedia pages, blogging, or keeping an online journal of sorts had replaced or at least changed the use of personal home pages. On the basis of these experiences, Web 2.0

emerged as a concept that outlined the principles for technology that would be built around users and their sociality and collaboration. The sociality and collaboration in the Web 2.0 model relied on one thing: connectivity—not only among users but also with the platform and its processes. The more connected and engaged the users were, the more these businesses were able to exploit from their interactions; the more intertwined the offline world became with the online world, the less room there was for disconnection.

The fundamentals of Web 2.0 also draw criticism focusing broadly on the aims at advocating the potential of users, participation, and collaboration and transforming these drives into a new mechanism of production and consumption. Tiziana Terranova problematized the notion of free labor to criticize some of the trends of the emergent network culture.[11] According to Terranova, "the sustainability of the Internet as a medium depends on massive amounts of labor," and yet this labor is not comparable to employment.[12] Terranova's notion is based on the assumption that the voluntary work that previously had a significant role in developing, distributing, and evaluating the core technologies of the internet was heightened and exploited extensively during the dot-com boom by different companies and turned into profit without compensation. She notes that, "of the incredible amount of labor that sustains the Internet as a whole (from mailing list traffic to Web sites to infrastructural questions), we can guess that a substantial amount of it is still 'free labor.'"[13]

It is against this background that we should evaluate social media alternatives and the ethicality of the disconnection they propose. For example, even if we buy the claims of Diaspora* and Ello, which state that "you are not a product!" and that these sites are not exploiting user information, we still have to critically approach their logic of enabling users. When Diaspora* or Ello invites users to disconnect from Facebook and join its own alternative, it is not offering an alternative business model from the perspective of participation. A diaspora is a people who are driven from their home and scattered but who still identify as a people. Similarly, the users of Diaspora* or Ello can be seen as people who have been driven from Facebook but who still identify with their community on social media—as opposed to just dropping out. Facebook alternatives buy into social media and the Web 2.0 logic of harnessing users to work through free collaboration and participation. While the data users contribute while participating are not sold, their participation is still as exploited as it is when they use other commercial social media sites. In both cases, users are producing what Michael Hardt and Antonio Negri call "immaterial products such as information, knowledge, ideas, images, relationships and affects"[14] within that particular social media platform. Users are tuning into the speeds and needs of participatory culture as neuroworkers,[15] regardless of the platform. There is no "pure" alternative to a financialized social media.

Detoxes

If quitting Facebook is as hard as quitting smoking, it would be easy to describe Facebook or any other social media platform as totalizing and deterministic. However, what constitutes its addictive capture also makes it fragile and vulnerable: the fact that Facebook builds on affective technosocial relationships. As Wendy Hui Kyong Chun points out, "the forms of control the Internet enables are not complete, and the freedom we experience stems from these controls; the forms of freedom the Internet enables stem from our vulnerabilities, from the fact that we do not entirely control our own actions."[16]

Throughout its history, Facebook has received criticism when its users have felt that they are no longer in control of what takes place on social media. For example, in November 2007, Facebook introduced a new function called Beacon. Beacon was part of Facebook's Ads system, and it was designed to connect Facebook users with forty-four commercial websites. Through this system, Facebook was planning to transform online purchases into sharable information; for example, her purchase of movie tickets would transform into information about a user's taste in movies, and this information could, according to Facebook, be beneficial for both other Facebook users and advertisers targeting their campaigns. A number of users, however, did not see Beacon as beneficial but rather as intrusive, and quickly, online activists formed a petition for Facebook to let them opt out from using Beacon. Facebook acknowledged their concerns, and participation in Beacon was made voluntary a month after its implementation.[17]

Another, more contemporary example that exposes users' vulnerabilities and the potential for exploitation is the 2017 confessions of

Chamath Palihapitiya, Facebook's former vice president of growth.[18] In an interview, Palihapitiya quite directly claimed that Facebook is addictive by design; it is built to engage users in a dopamine-driven feedback loop, and this is destroying how society works. Thus Palihapitiya does not let his children use Facebook and recommends that people take a break from Facebook.[19]

The solution for reclaiming our lives seems simple: we need to *disconnect* from social media. Building directly on the idea of our social media connections being addictive and users being vulnerable is the digital detox movement. The idea of digital detox is easy as pie: when we disconnect from our social media sources, such as laptops, mobile devices, tablets, and computers, we can use that time for doing whatever we really enjoy. The eponymous business venture Digital Detox is an example of this growing industry currently being built around services that offer us ways to unplug:

> We are more globally connected than ever before, but life in the digital age is far from ideal. The average American spends more than half of their waking life staring at a screen. The negative psychological, social and cultural impact is real. Things need to change. . . . In an era of constant technological acceleration and innovation, an over abundance of screen time, information overload, tech-driven anxiety, social media everything, internet addiction, a constant sense of FOMO (fear of missing out), selfies, and being endlessly tethered and always available—many have referred to us as the ultimate decelerator.[20]

Disconnection for Digital Detox is a commodity that has an increasing amount of demand. It sees disconnection as something that can be supplied through retreats and camps where simple practices, such as taking away personal technological devices, are used. "As we *disconnect* from our devices, we *reconnect* with ourselves, our community, nature and the world at large," Digital Detox declares.[21] The marketing lingo of Digital Detox frames our user relation as problematic and offers a way to buy out from the situation by joining a retreat or a summer camp where the problems are solved by removing digital devices. Digital Detox wants to reduce disconnection into a function of a simple on–off mechanism. For Digital Detox, disconnection equals the nonuse of social media technologies.

Disconnection, however, is not simply about switching on or off but, as Laura Portwood-Stacer notes, is in general a question of affordances.[22] Portwood-Stacer examines users who *consciously* choose *not* to engage with social media. The reasons for refusal range, for example, from platform-specific problems, such as frustration with the site's interface or privacy policy, to questions of being more productive when social media do not demand that much time.[23] According to Portwood-Stacer, disconnection is a political performance through personal practices but also a way to express social capital.[24] The capability to disconnect implies that the offline social network is so strong that the user does not need to participate in online social networks.

Both Digital Detox and the people interviewed by Portwood-Stacer stress the distinction between the online and the offline, between Facebook and the real or terrestrial world. The fear of missing out produced by tying offline networks with social media platforms shows how online and offline have become indistinguishably intermixed. Thus, social media, as Jose van Dijck reminds us, not only enable relationships but can also disable them:

> Once a member, the social push to stay connected is insidious,
> especially for young people, because *not* being on Facebook means
> not being invited to parties, not getting updated on important
> events, in short, being disconnected from a presumably appealing
> dynamic of public life.[25]

Choosing to use or not to use social media is one of the possible choices for users, but as Ben Light shows, there are multiple and more nuanced ways in which "disconnective practices" are part of our online relationships.[26] These involve, for example, choosing who one "friends" and "unfriends" on Facebook and whose status updates one decides to follow or hide; social media users can disconnect within the platform as well.[27]

Control and freedom in the context of social media culminates in the attempts to disconnect. Palihapithya and the Digital Detox movement ague that we as users are vulnerable to social media platforms and as such are not in control of our use. The solution to disconnect is extreme, but it is also the only possible way to resist the dominance of social media over our lives. However, the aforementioned approaches by Light and Portwood-Stacer give us a more nuanced understanding of user agency in this context. Both Portwood-Stacer and Light map the different ways users use disconnection to reflect on, conceptualize, and make sense of their relationships with social media and other users. Disconnection is not only a question of control but is also a question of freedom, not as total abstention or nonuse but as a qualitative difference in connection. Connecting and disconnecting are affective forces that shape a user's online and offline social relationships and are frustrated by the complex interrelationships that develop between a user's online and real-world social networks but also between the platform and its functions.

Experiments

As the contemporary discussion often highlights, social media platforms are not neutral, but they enable and manage different things while disabling others. Social media platforms are part of sociotechnological diagrams that have the power to filter "which cultural discourses and non-discursive practices emerge."[28] According to Tarleton Gillespie, the platform is a "'raised level surface' designed to facilitate some activity that will subsequently take place."[29] Ganaele Langlois makes a similar argument worth quoting at length here:

> The common feature of all participatory media platforms is that they not only allow users to express themselves by enabling content transmission, but also establish the customized networked conditions within which something can become culturally meaningful and shareable. The platform acts as a manager that enables, directs, and channels specific flows of communication as well as specific logics of transformation of data into culturally recognizable and valuable signs and symbols. Thus, it is useful to think about participatory media platforms as conduits for governance, that is, as the conduits that actualize technocultural assemblages, and therefore manage a field of communicational processes, practices, and expectations through specific articulations between hardware, software, and users.[30]

The notion of Facebook being a manager of certain flows of communication and having mechanisms in place that influence what messages become heard has been highlighted in the context of the U.S.

presidential election of 2016. Especially the ongoing debate related to fake news and the speculations of the influence of foreign countries in the election have put the role of Facebook in the vulnerability of our connectivity under examination. Facebook has in fact acknowledged that the platform may have been used to influence opinions through ads. According to Facebook's chief security officer, Alex Stamos, during the elections, inauthentic user accounts that "likely operated out of Russia" spent $100,000 to send three thousand Facebook ads.[31] The same report maintains that the

> vast majority of ads run by these accounts didn't specifically reference the US presidential election, voting or a particular candidate. Rather, the ads and accounts appeared to focus on amplifying divisive social and political messages across the ideological spectrum—touching on topics from LGBT matters to race issues to immigration to gun rights.[32]

In the case of the presidential elections, we see at least speculation of how social media sites allow different "connection strategies" and how they can be effectively used to shape opinions.[33] Advertisers and everyday users are not equal. For example, on Twitter, through APIs, some advertisers can use historical and real-time data and proprietary natural language processing and learning algorithms to find audiences for their messages and better target advertising campaigns.[34] The platform has an important role in connectivity, and disconnections are built within its protocological assemblages.[35] Arguably, then, the case of using Facebook ads to influence opinion is not an anomaly but is rather what the platform was designed to do.

Kate Crawford argues that attention should also be paid to the "political spaces in which algorithms function, are produced, and modified."[36] On October 6, 2017, the *Guardian* ran a story titled "'Our Minds Can Be Hijacked': The Tech Insiders Who Fear a Smartphone Dystopia."[37] The story was about Google, Twitter, and Facebook workers who designed features such as Facebook's Like button and are now disconnecting themselves from the internet and the social media sites they helped to build. The story describes how these workers and other tech people are hiring employees to manage their Facebook pages so that they do not have to engage with them; are sending their children to schools where iPhones and laptops are banned; and are installing "an outlet timer connected to a router that cuts off access to the internet at a set time every day."[38]

These techniques of disconnection are used, according to tech consultant Nir Eyal, to remind us that we are still in control of our social media use.[39] We are here reminded of Deleuze, who famously pairs choice with control in the modern apparatuses of power.[40] Deleuze's argument is that the subject does not need to be confined to be controlled; control is not a discipline. Instead, Deleuze proposes a model where the means of control are multiplied to the extent that the subject experiences control as an infinite freedom of choice while in fact all these choices are perfectly controlled.[41] For Raiford Guins, new media technologies work with the same logic. They enable a wide range of different choices while simultaneously demarcating others. This freedom of choice is not a real choice but rather a mode of action administered and managed through new media technologies.[42] According to Guins, there is a double pull where control mechanisms are embedded in media technologies but, simultaneously, control is discursively placed in the hands of the users themselves as a choice and responsibility of using these technologies in a certain way.[43] A corollary of this is, of course, the number of applications and technologies designed to make users feel productive by disconnecting their social media feeds.[44]

Patricia Clough maintains that control no longer tries to produce particular subjects but "aims at a never-ending modulation of moods, capacities, affects, and potentialities."[45] The aforementioned story in the *Guardian* frames the Facebook Like button as an example of the illusion of being in control while we are in fact not. In the story, the tale of the invention of Facebook's Like button is told by one of its developers, Justin Rosenstein; according to him, the Like button was designed to spread positive vibes on the platform but resulted in the production of "pseudo-pleasure."[46] The social media critics in the same news report describe engagement with social media as an addictive feedback loop, which is not accidental but rather one of the platforms' in-built features. For example, Eyal, in the *Guardian* story, argues that "the technologies we use have turned into compulsions. . . . It's the pull to visit YouTube, Facebook, or Twitter for just a few minutes, only to find yourself still tapping and scrolling an hour later."[47] To talk about compulsion is to imply that we are forced to connect and are psychologically incapable of disconnecting.

The example of the Like button or the description of feedback loops, however, is important here not as a description of psychological processes of controlling social media users but as an example of affective modulation that keeps users engaged. Affective modulation is not deterministic, structured, or clearly definable; rather, it is control through the constitution of a field of possibilities that can actualize or become actualized through different means. In the aforementioned Guardian story, affective modulation is described through how social media sites could recognize emotional vulnerabilities, such as feelings of being insecure, bored, lonely, or frustrated, and then exploit these moments by triggering "mindless action to quell the negative sensation."[48] This is an example of affective modulation. This is what Massumi calls "the infra-level where the individual is emergently divided among potential inflections of its own self-formative movements."[49]

Whereas the *Guardian* story speculates about the idea of affective modulation as a form of control, we have an example where Facebook has directly experimented with users' emotions. In 2014, a group of Facebook-affiliated researchers published a highly controversial study titled "Experimental Evidence of Massive-Scale Emotional Contagion through Social Networks."[50] According to this study, "emotional states can be transferred to others via emotional contagion, leading them to experience the same emotions as those around them" and Facebook News Feed is the "product" through which users most often express their emotions.[51] From this hypothesis, the researchers argued that Facebook manipulating the visibility of News Feed content could transfer users' emotional states from user to user. To be clear, this study was not theoretical but empirical. Researchers tested their hypothesis with 689,003 Facebook users by reducing either negatively or positively loaded content from their News Feeds. They noticed that reducing negative content from the News Feed post would also reduce the negativity from the content users who saw the post would post, and vice versa. Emotional contagion happened without the users ever being aware of being subjected to a test.[52]

The controversy around this experiment was caused by the fact that Facebook users were not aware of being subjects of human research. By referring to Facebook's data use policy, the researchers argued that users had consigned Facebook the authority to conduct this or any other type of research, and because the experiment was "conducted by Facebook, Inc. for internal purposes," it "did not fall under Cornell's Human Research Protection Program."[53] While the focus of the critique was on using users as research subjects, from my point of view, what is much more interesting is how user engagement with the platform was exploited to affect the connected users.

To talk about the experiment as an example of affective modulation rather than an example of psychological or emotional control is to connect it with the theorization of affect, which in cultural studies has become a key framework to understand the forces of encounter or passages between bodies that are not fully reducible to things like meaning, semiotics, or rational and cognitive processes. Through this approach, our user engagements with social media sites are seen as relations where humans are affected by various "events prior to and independent of their cognitive impact or interpretation."[54] Understandings of affect, as Gregory J. Seigworth and Melissa Gregg point out, are divided into two different main trends invoked in two separate essays in 1995, one by Brian Massumi ("The Autonomy of Affect") and one by Eve Sedgwick and Adam Frank ("Shame in the Cybernetic Fold").[55] The former is grounded in Deleuze's poststructuralist conception of the affect, while the latter was inspired by a reading of Silvan Tomkins's interpretation of differential affects.

The followers of the Tomkins line consider affects as bodily emotions that emerge as bodily responses to triggering objects without meaning or association to the source as such;[56] affects connect us to other objects and place us in the circuit of feeling and response through which the outside world is experienced.[57] It is easy to interpret Facebook's emotional contagion study from this view. Particular emotions were triggered by increasing or decreasing negative content on users' Facebook News Feeds.

Massumi and his followers, in contrast, understand affects as passages between different states that are neither personal nor emotional. Affects precede emotions. Massumi understands affects as intensities that have not yet been raised to the level of emotion. Affects are intensities that do not belong to the body but take place during moments of affection, and when you affect something, you also open yourself up to being affected. What takes place is a transition of the body, however slight that might be.[58] Affects for Massumi, in contrast to Tomkins, work at an abstract level of becoming that need not be reduced to human psychology. In fact, the question is no longer about the human body and its emotions at all, but affectivity takes place literally between *any body,* human or nonhuman.[59] This any body is an assemblage of force relations, and the power of being affected determines how such assemblages may take place.[60]

The difference between these two takes on affect also suggests two different understandings of the social media user as subject. The study of emotional contagion on Facebook equates affect with emotion. In this model, emotions, though triggered by the News Feed, belong to the users and are experiences that can be recognized and shared. The Massumian approach, however, gives a different spectrum with which to work. Massumi himself mentions Facebook's experiment briefly when he talks about affect:

> It is as easy as click-bait to modulate that ebb and flow [of infrahuman flows of desire, tendency, fear, hope, self-interest, sympathy, tensings for action and easings into relation] in order to orient its taking-determinate-form. Facebook demonstrated this with its infamous informal experiment in modulating people's moods and online behavior by modulating the affective tenor of their Facebook feeds.[61]

From the Massumian perspective, Facebook's emotional contagion study can be seen as a study of how technological platforms can be used to control and modulate intensities on a presubjective level. In the case of the emotional contagion study, what is interesting is no longer one particular status update and the increasing or decreasing of its negative or positive value but the overall system that is capable of modulating and distributing affects. Thus, when Mark Zuckerberg describes Facebook as "the most powerful distribution mechanism that's been created in a generation,"[62] we should not understand it merely as a mechanism of posting photos or other user-generated content that may affect other users but also as a mechanism that is capable of opening a person up to being affected in turn.

If we follow the Massumian understanding of affect, Facebook constitutes an intensive field or field of intensity, which can be used to modulate and produce the flow of needs, demands, and desires for the users of the platform. This field modulates what Paasonen et al. call "the fluctuating and altering dynamics of affect," which "give shape to online connections and disconnections."[63] In other words, platforms like Facebook and Twitter come between resonating bodies as mediators producing and directing the flow of affect.[64] These platforms establish connections among people and things: we see users' posts on News Feed; we can chat with them and send private messages on Messenger; we can even choose how much content we want to see from particular friends by marking them as "close friends" or "acquaintances." Algorithms intensify these relationships.

Facebook has for a while now used a particular algorithm to control the visibility of posts based, for example, on our previous interactions with particular Facebook friends.[65] Twitter made a similar change to its Timeline in 2016 and is now also using an algorithm that chooses and shows first a tweet that a user is "likely to care about most" by applying information such as which users the person interacts with most, which tweets she engages with, "and much more."[66] What we see in these features is not the frictionless flow of real time information but instead a modulation of affective streams. When we become affected by posts and tweets, the platforms register our interactions. These data are used to build, maintain, and establish a frictionless experience based on stronger or weaker relations; the more we interact with a particular person, the more posts or tweets from that person will be shown us. Our interactions with the platform enter into a never-ending loop of modulation.

When we read the study "Experimental Evidence of Massive-Scale Emotional Contagion through Social Networks"[67] through affect, we begin to see how social media are much more than instruments or tools for social exchange. Social media are a factory of affect that actively configures the interactions and encounters happening on the platform.[68] This modulation happens in many ways and through different methods. Following Paasonen, user agency means intimate cohabitation with multiple and heterogeneous devices and networks, which are oriented by, and give rise to, our experiences, sensations, and perceptions.[69] Terranova makes a very similar observation when she argues that information technology has the capability to inform our habits and percepts and that information architectures shape and produce our reality "in a way that does not only involve our capacity to signify—that is, to know the world through a system of signs."[70] This modulation happens in addition to and sometimes at the expense of users as rational subjects actively making decisions based on cognitive evaluations.

Hence it becomes important to ask which modalities of disconnection belong to the field of user agency on social media, which are implicated by it, and which escape it. Reason, rationality, and purposefulness, to paraphrase Zizi Papacharissi, are not adequate frameworks for understanding either our social media connections or our disconnections.[71] User agency as a model enabled, designed, and modulated by the platform is "ambivalent connectivity to and dependency on various networks" rather than "rational and instrumental control over technology," Paasonen underlines.[72] Reason, rationality, or arguments about instrumentality do not provide an understanding of why we decide *not* to disconnect. This critique of rationality does not place the user in the position of a passive subject but is intended to explicate that on social media, affective involvements are constantly taking place that cannot be rationally or instrumentally explained. Paraphrasing Coté, if rational thought occurs, it occurs "in this assemblage of human and technics imbued with and typically predisposed by sub-perceptual affect."[73] The social media platform is a relay of social and technical, human and nonhuman, tied together with affective intensities. We as users may think we are savvy about the value our attention and engagement create, as Jenkins et al. posit,[74] but study of emotional/affective contagion implies, in contrast, that we are not in control even of our attention and engagement. While social media platforms are effective technologies for spreading messages, they also guide our attention and maneuver us to think about and desire certain things instead of others.[75] The desire to disconnect is hardly what these platforms want to produce.

Designs

Ben Light and Elijah Cassidy highlight that Facebook "deploys disconnection" to stabilize social media arrangements so that "any threat to the company's existence through mass exodus is averted."[76] Here the word *disconnection* indicates both action and the agency from the user side and a state of existence that can be maintained and created from the platform side.[77] Dealing with disconnections thus means dealing with the potential, the possible, the probable. According to

Light and Cassidy, it is about allowing disconnections, "but only on very particular socioeconomic terms."[78]

Disconnections add an element of uncertainty to the designs of social media platforms. In other words, disconnection is a principle that social media platforms need to take into account. Designing against disconnections is to try to make the possibility of disconnection disappear. In this fashion, disconnections premediate connections.[79] Grusin explains:

> premediation deploys multiple modes of mediation and remediation in shaping the affectivity of the public, in preparing people for some field of possible future actions, in producing a mood or structure of feeling that makes possible certain kinds of actions, thoughts, speech, affectivities, feelings, or moods, mediations that might not have seemed possible before or that might have fallen flat or died on the vine or not produced echoes and reverberations in the public or media sphere.[80]

For Grusin, premediation describes how different media try to anticipate "the future not as it emerges immediately into the present but before it ever happens" and make sure that "when the future comes it has already been remediated."[81] Premediation happens with a double logic where, on one hand, the future is already produced before it happens and, on the other hand, at the very moment when the future emerges into the present, it becomes captured by media technologies.

Grusin's notion of premediation describes a political and cultural climate beginning with 9/11 and moving toward the current state of affairs where preemptive strikes have become accepted foreign policy measures and reactions to different threats that have not yet actualized. As Brian Massumi also describes, a preemptive strike does not need a clear and present danger for justification but is used in eliminating a threat that inhabits the future.[82] To preempt a threat is to respond rapidly to what has not yet emerged. Massumi notes that threat and preemption indicate a time loop where "the future comes back to the present to trigger a reaction that jolts the present back to the future, along a different path of action than would have eventuated otherwise."[83] According to Mark Andrejevic, preemption is not only about destroying or preventing through opposition but also about setting goals that are both preemptive and productive—on one hand, to preempt means to minimize negative impacts and, on the other hand, to maximize emotional investment and engagement.[84]

Premediation is preemption's media-specific strategy. The question is no longer only about war or foreign politics but more generally about the cultural logic that is also inscribed in the functions of our current social media technologies. Manifestations of this logic are, for example, recommendation algorithms designed to predict your interests and offer you things you might like to see. Often these algorithms are surrounded with a veil of secrecy. Frank Pasquale calls them "black boxes," as they seem to govern our world, but we do not know exactly how or according to which principles.[85] Netflix has algorithms that predict what movies you want to watch. The financial world uses algorithms for automated trading. Google uses the PageRank algorithm to determine search results based on users' previous engagements. But algorithms that decide search results are also reflecting and reinstantiating "the current social climate and prevailing social and cultural values" of, for example, sexism and racism, as Safiya Umoja Noble's work on racialized and gendered identities has shown.[86] Algorithms are productive as much as they are predictive. "Facebook will market you your future before you've even gotten there, they'll use predictive algorithms to figure out what's your likely future and then try to make that even more likely," Douglas Rushkoff polemically argues.[87] If the companies get to decide, disconnection, most likely, is neither the future that becomes predicted nor the future that becomes produced.

Another example of premediating disconnections is the expansion of ways to use Facebook. As Portwood-Stacer points out, Facebook's social and economic value is tied not only to its users but also to its capability to expand; Facebook's "business model is premised upon ubiquity to the point of naturalization—it seeks to become thoroughly integrated into the fabric of everyday life for as many people as possible, to the extent that they cannot imagine life without it and thus do not think to question its presence in their lives."[88] In *The Facebook Effect,* David Kirkpatrick points out that "it's been a joke around the Facebook offices for years that the company seeks 'total domination,'" but in fact, Zuckerberg realized early on that "people will join and use the communications tool that the largest number of other people are using."[89] This observation has led the company to use an aggressive global expansion strategy. As Kirkpatrick argues, Facebook's "objective was to overwhelm all other social networks wherever they are—to win their users and become the de facto standard. In his [Zuckerberg] view it was either that or disappear."[90]

In recent years, we have seen that becoming ubiquitous has been Facebook's way to answer the problem of disconnection. Facebook has moved from the screens of personal computers to mobile devices, television receivers, video game consoles, and GPS navigators. It seems that Facebook will be integrated with every conceivable device and gadget sooner or later. With an in-vehicle integration one's car dashboard can display Facebook conversations. Moreover, Facebook is integrated with different websites, services, and technologies. Research done by the web monitoring service Pingdom in 2013 points out that 24.3 percent of the top ten thousand websites have some kind of official Facebook interaction.[91] Basically, this means that users are engaged with Facebook through these integrations, even though they may not think they are using Facebook at that very moment. Importantly, this expansion or colonization happens within Facebook. Facebook co-opts traditional media, such as movies, television, and newspapers, within its own system. Facebook Watch is a video-on-demand service that hosts original programming. Facebook has augmented reality tools one can use to leave messages and notes to the real world accessible through their service. Facebook Spaces is how the company is imagining virtual reality: as an environment where one can have Messenger video calls and post content live on friends' Facebook streams.

"Disconnection . . . augments rather than corrupts Facebook," Light and Cassidy remark.[92] Terranova maintains that this expansive logic of digital social networks has a longer history in the context of governing masses and establishing techniques of control.[93] Like Portwood-Stacer, Terranova maintains that social media build on the "capacity to ensure an expansive circulation integrating more and more elements within its circuits."[94] The more social media expand, the less possibility there is for loss or error. Hence Facebook colonizes our networked environment. The proposition of the expansion of material devices, ubiquitous computing, and pervasive media is that for users to be engaged, they need not go anywhere or do anything special. They are connected anywhere and everywhere. The social media are with them, in their pockets, in their cars, in the devices they carry with them. The mobile version of Facebook is always on checking for new interactions. Facebook becoming ubiquitous in and through material devices points toward a situation where we are engaged almost without a choice.[95] When Facebook fertilizes/permeates our everyday environment, being on Facebook, being engaged all the time, becomes a naturalized state of being and disconnection as a choice dissipates.

For social media companies, connectivity is an absolute value. Social media sites argue that through connectivity, societies can change and people can become liberated.[96] Grusin highlights the ideal of connectivity as an absolute value through premediation:

> Social networks exist for the purpose of premediating connectivity, by promoting an anticipation that a connection will be made—that somebody will comment on your blog or your Facebook profile or respond to your Tweet, that you will hear the distinctive ringtone of one of your favorites, that your computer or your networked phone will alert you that you have new mail or that you have been texted. These anticipated connections, however, are not determined or specified in any particular way. It is connectivity itself that one anticipates, not necessarily a specific connection.[97]

Connectivity as an absolute value suggests that the overall capability to connect is more important than the nature or quality of the connections.

To recap, if the noun *disconnect* denotes the instance of disconnecting or being disconnected, it is this definition the principle of overall connectivity wants to eliminate in its entirety. Desires to disconnect produce a paradox, because they justify the social media company to take anticipatory measures and build new ways to engage users even more deeply in the processes and practices the platform mediates. Arguably, disconnection, when it becomes a problem for the platform, does not weaken connections but makes them stronger, because the problem of disconnection needs to be solved. Yet disconnection is always present, also with enabling overall connectivity. Perhaps it lurks only in the form of discrepancy of connection, as the second definition of the noun states. To point out these discrepancies is the work of critical social media studies. The discrepancy between users and the platform, when connected, cannot be forgotten.

Postscripts

I have discussed users and their agency in relation to social media, but I want to conclude with another framework where disconnection becomes an issue of nation-states. Between January 27 and 28, 2011, the government of Egypt tried to shut down the country's internet traffic almost entirely to control ongoing protests related to the so-called Arab Spring.[98] Conceptually, the Arab Spring describes the uprisings and protests that began in Tunisia in 2009 and spread widely to neighboring areas. The role of social media in the events of the Arab Spring, both before and after this disconnection, has gained much attention both in the public and within academia. According to a research team led by Phillip N. Howard, "social media played a central role in shaping political debates in the Arab Spring."[99] Howard et al. show in particular how young urban and well-educated crowds used Facebook, Twitter, and YouTube in the Arab world to disseminate political messages and put pressure on governments. Through social media, news from the region and from international media outlets was spread, often across international borders.[100]

The role of social media in the Arab Spring is noticeable not only because it connected and empowered people but also because disconnection was used as a political tool to control the people. According to Paasonen, the uncertainty, helplessness, and lack of agency in being a social media user reveal themselves in the moments when users are "being cut off from the multiple networks that modify the possibilities of engaging with the surrounding world."[101] When Egypt shut down internet traffic, users were no longer in control of their social media use. Rather, they were controlled by their inability to access the platforms. Participants in the Arab Spring had counted on Facebook's call on its users to participate; they were trusting Facebook to grant its users "the power to share" and thus "make the world more open and connected," but the diagram of power shifted when access to the networks and social media platforms was forbidden and the state took control through its power to disconnect users.

This break, however, as Manuel Castells notes, was only temporary. It lasted five days, and during those days, people started finding alternative ways to connect. They were using fax machines, ham radios, dial-up connections, and landline telephones to communicate. Systems that translated voicemail messages into tweets were incorporated. A complete shutdown became impossible.[102]

The five-day disconnect makes a point Friedrich Kittler and numerous new materialistic critics have tried to make for more than a decade: that digital media cannot be reduced to the mere operations of the software, the immaterial, the digital. Social media platforms also have an infrastructure. This infrastructure of connectivity is subject to politics, or better, as Howard, Agarwal, and Hussain state, "information infrastructure *is* politics"—it enables particular forms of governance and control.[103] For example, access to the internet goes through a global submarine cable network, and its operations run in numerous data centers both owned and leased by different companies, and this access may be controlled by state-controlled corporations.[104] Or the state can order internet service providers to shut off access to the internet by deleting IP addresses, as, according to Castells, Egypt did.[105] The infrastructure of the internet allows both connections and disconnections.

But perhaps an even more important thing the five day-disconnect reveals is that the bonds between connections and disconnections are always also economical. Massumi carves this into a philosophical formula: "capitalism has learned to motorize itself immanently to its own movements."[106] Egypt's reason to restore access to the internet was very much financial: the shutdown was costing money for the government, resulting, according to Castells, in a loss of approximately $90 million in revenue. All connections seem to connect to networked capitalism, and it is this network against which disconnection does not seem to stand a chance. "The Internet is the lifeline of the interconnected global economy, and so its disconnection can only be exceptional and for a limited period of time," Castells notes.[107]

Log Out

On October 18, 2010, the *Wall Street Journal* published a story titled "Facebook in Privacy Breach."[1] According to the story, a number of Facebook applications were "transmitting identifying information—in effect, providing access to people's names and, in some cases, their friends' names—to dozens of advertising and Internet tracking companies."[2] These applications were operating against Facebook's rules and policies against sharing identifiable user information with third parties. As soon as the privacy breach was reported, Facebook took action to disable all applications that violated its terms of service. The breach had, however, already happened, raising the question of Facebook's ability to keep identifiable information about its users' activities secure and adding fuel to the fire of movements such as Quit Facebook Day.[3]

This breach not only expresses the vulnerabilities of Facebook but also brings us to the problems of privacy from the perspective of the platform and social media businesses. This problem, as Wendy Hui Kyong Chun has expressed, is that "Internet users . . . are framed as private subjects exposed in public," and in this process, the private is being privatized and reduced to secrecy and corporate security.[4] She argues that in our understandings of social networks, we rely on models that preceded social media sites and take them as private and personal. What follows is an inherent incompatibility when this understanding is translated and collapsed with the nonpersonal, nonhuman networks of computational systems.[5] Whereas Chun suggests that to tackle this problem, we need to see privacy as doing publicity and develop public rights,[6] our surrounding culture of connectivity has a different solution: privacy can be governed and controlled via an app.

There is indeed a software application like this, which the *New York Times* chose as its "favorite privacy tool" and which currently "empower[s] over 50 million people to protect their privacy, security and device performance."[7] I am of course referring here to Disconnect, a corporation with an eponymous privacy software app. The development of this app is directly connected to the aforementioned Facebook privacy breach. Concerned about the breach, a former Google engineer, Brian Kennish, wrote a piece of software called Facebook Disconnect.[8] The software was designed to stop Facebook from tracking users' movements around the Web. Facebook Disconnect quickly gained attention from the press, and Kennish kept working with the software. In December 2010, a new version, called Disconnect, was launched. Disconnect focused on blocking the data mining of a number of social media sites, including Facebook and Twitter, but it also targeted search engines, which were storing users' searches. When installed, Disconnect blocks malware and hidden requests for information that could leave one vulnerable to privacy and security threats. It makes the mining of information visible by showing users the number of trackers and identifying the sources.

Disconnect does not delete a user's online presence, but it blocks an important portion of it. Websites that make money from allowing advertisers and analytics companies to track users and then serve targeted ads based on these actions become obstructed by the app. Disconnect interrupts these data flows often commoditized by marketing agencies and advertisers and drives a wedge between our everyday social and cultural practices taking place online and the ways in which these relations and practices are being monetized.

Disconnect does not disconnect but rather blocks and prevents and, while doing so, adds another layer of privatization and technologization of privacy. However, Disconnect also turns privacy into a product that has a price. Although the basic version is free, both the Pro and Premium versions come with a cost and offer more speed and less bandwidth. Premium also offers a Virtual Network Service to hide the user's IP address. Disconnect is not the only service to suggest a pay-for-privacy model. AT&T and Comcast have plans to offer lower prices to their broadband users if they are willing to be served targeted ads based on their internet browsing histories; privacy becomes a luxury item for people willing and able to pay.[9]

Privacy is not only an issue of technology but also of logics of an economy. Pay-for-privacy models implemented through technology give us a neoliberal understanding of privacy. Under this framework, as Chun points out, everything can be analyzed in terms of cost and benefits.[10] The market becomes the entity that empowers the individual to reclaim their privacy. Disconnect, then, not only challenges advertisers or marketers but illustrates how connections, disconnections, and privacy are captured by the economy.

Users

"Every connection has its price; the one thing you can be sure of is that, sooner or later, you will have to pay," Steven Shaviro polemically argues.[11] One of these prices is the decentralization of the human subject by the social media platform and the introduction of mechanisms that condition users' possibilities toward becoming a commodity. Apps such as Disconnect may protect us from involuntary sharing of data, but they cannot protect us against the constant processes of "self-production" or "self-branding,"[12] whereby we paint a picture of ourselves not only to our peer users but also for the social media platform and its codes, algorithms, and other marketing mechanisms. This voluntary content production—a name that does not do justice to the heterogeneous activities users have on social media—is always a process of becoming a particular node that can be simultaneously identified and modeled. On social media, the user is both singular and plural, as Chun argues; social media make users part of a big data drama, where their actions are captured and even their silences are registered and analyzed in comparison to others they resemble.[13]

This can happen through sophisticated systems of capture, where information is not extracted from us by force but we have rather desired to share it ourselves. For example, since 2011, correlating with the launch of the Timeline interface, Facebook users have been able to add and make visible important moments happening in their lives. According to Facebook's Help Center, the "*Life Event* option lets you add experiences from the different parts of your life to your Timeline. Life Events are divided into categories (ex: Work & Education,

Family & Relationships), and you can use them to share many different kinds of important moments, from an engagement or trip to a new baby or home."[14] Basically, a user is able to choose from different categories a specific life event, such as buying a car, getting married, or losing weight; post that event on Facebook; and store it on his Timeline. Life Events establishes the conditions for what Sari Östman calls "life-publishing," illustrating how posting on social media reflects users' own identities but also constitutes a performance for an audience.[15] Facebook's Life Events are both discursive and nondiscursive practices. Maurizio Lazzarato explains: "nondiscursive dispositifs or practices intervene in what one does (possible or probable action), whilst discursive practices or dispositifs intervene in what one says (possible or probable statements)."[16] With Life Events, Facebook is giving us a list of events that it considers significant to users' lives. By defining these events, Facebook simultaneously constructs and determines the importance of certain moments or events over others.

Posting a Life Event connects users to a network of Facebook-specific procedures, protocols, and actions. These nondiscursive practices, run by, for example, the EdgeRank algorithm, determine how visible events will be for other users.[17] Simultaneously, they connect user information to data policies and ways to target advertisements based on what is happening in the user's life. Life Events is a Facebook-specific materialization of identity and affect for the means of value production. For the platform, adding a Life Event constructs what Alexander Galloway calls an *affective identity marker*.[18] The use of these affective identity markers for marketing is explained on the Facebook for Business site:

> Trying to boost sales at your flower shop? It's now easier to reach people who have recently declared their love for someone on Facebook. Core Audiences features more values for relationship status (like civil unions and domestic partnerships) as well as timely changes in life events, like getting engaged or married.[19]

On the basis of this information, posting a life event, such as getting married, codifies the user into a certain demographic category, which is then used, for example, for selling flowers. As Mark Coté and Jennifer Pybus have noted, affective engagements bring users and networked relations together and help "forge relationships . . . through new subjectivities and networked relations that have the potential to interpolate users for the various lifestyles and identities that are being produced on an on-going basis."[20] Galloway sees this relation as deterministic; the body (or the user) has no other choice than to represent that certain demographic category whatever it does online. In fact, he notes that there is always an algorithm listening somewhere and that the connected body speaks because it does not have any other choice.[21]

This production and conditioning of users by the platform is future oriented; it exceeds a user's current individual characteristics and enters the domain of a user's interests and affinities. When John Cheney-Lippold talks about "algorithmic identities," he refers to the way Web analytic companies identify users based on their Web-surfing habits. Importantly, these companies do not just describe their users; they also produce or model these users.[22] On one hand, social media companies have created machines of capture, such as Life Events, to intensify processes of identification and social formation, but on the other hand, under the hood of the interface, Facebook uses this information to manipulate the future potential.

This potential, if we think about social media as a business, is obviously economic. We are constantly being targeted online by advertisers who are interested in the sites we visit and the things to which we show attachment. On the basis of the information we give out, we are being computationally profiled. This profiling leads to decisions and judgments, such as what ads are offered to us, and these judgments are computationally made through "the imaginative calculation of the possibility, and not the strict probability, of a future event."[23] Cheney-Lippold notes that algorithmic identity is inferred by using statistical commonality models to determine one's gender, class, or race in an automatic manner, and at the same time, these measures define the meaning of gender, class, or race themselves.[24] Cheney-Lippold argues that this produces a paradox. The algorithmic identity put together by analytics is not an actual representation of us but rather an artificial construct based on our online habits. We are pushed toward these identities by platform-specific means that condition the ways we use social media.[25]

Facebook offers us the possibility to download our own Facebook data, and by looking at what is included, we can get an impression of what is being mined and how we are being profiled. While the data

Facebook gives us are not a complete collection of all our actions and relations on Facebook, they do illustrate the vastness of information constantly collected. According to Facebook, the data set "includes a lot of the same information available to you in your account and activity log, including your Timeline info, posts you have shared, messages, photos and more. Additionally, it includes information that is not available simply by logging into your account, like the ads you have clicked on, data like the IP addresses that are logged when you log into or out of Facebook, and more."[26]

These data can be part of not only our algorithmic identities but also what Louise Amoore defines as *data derivatives*.[27] Amoore takes the idea of data derivatives from the financial definition of "derivative instruments" as forms of "risk management in which the relationship between the instrument and an assumed underlying value becomes fleeting, uncertain and loose."[28] Derivatives instruments, such as options, futures, swaps, and forwards, try to derive assets' future values based on observable components, including price, interest rates, exchange rates, and indexes. They slice and rebundle these values to make the future predictable. Similarly, social media data mining extracts data from users and hashes the data to make the actual identities disappear. Then they aggregate and analyze the data and push them back to users in the form of premediated futures. According to Amoore, "the data derivative is not centered on who we are, nor even on what our data says about us, but on what can be imagined and inferred about who we might be—on our very proclivities and potentialities."[29]

Data have allowed social media platforms to become a "data broker" connecting online and offline worlds. Here, again, Facebook is an example. The company recently acquired Atlas, a tool for online advertisers to track how online ads materialize in offline purchases. According to *Wired*, Atlas has the technology to match the phone numbers and email addresses of Facebook users with the "phone numbers and email addresses consumers provide in stores."[30] When you buy something from a store and give the store your phone number or email, that purchase can be tracked and a correlation between you seeing the product online and then making the purchase offline can be shown. In short, Atlas is a tool to track how the online affects the offline, and vice versa. Here you are not only purchasing the product but become involved in a much more entangled processes of affective capitalism that no longer makes a separation between the online and the offline.

New tools like Atlas or Internet.org and the integration of Facebook with a user's smartphone, smart television, car, video game console, or any device that offers online connectivity are tactics of expansion and part of an economic logic that aims to ensure that a user remains engaged with the platform and simultaneously keeps on producing data. Social media are becoming connected to everything, but also the converse happens: everything becomes connected to social media. Marketing and advertising are only one part of these connections. According to Amoore, social network analysis assembles pieces of data from otherwise unrelated databases, such as chat rooms, online transactions, and websites. These data are then used by Homeland Security to spot possible terrorist networks.[31] The mining of social media data has become an industry, and different actors, such as financial traders, use social media data to predict what will happen in the stock markets and to act preemptively.[32] The data sets assembled from our social media use are huge, and the connections they enable are sometimes unexpected.

There is a movement to track here, where users, understood as algorithmic identities, and user data, understood as a derivative, form the basis of economic value. This is a value that operates on futurity and the possible rather than the present and actual. As Adam Arvidsson has argued, the economic value of social media is tied to "making probabilistic interferences from data gathered from their [users'] movements and activities, and acting on these."[33] The platform's value is in the possible futures it claims to be able to predict and produce through connectivity. Again, consider targeted marketing. The correlation of particular data points, such as age, location, and the recent purchase of a movie ticket, can be used to calculate a possible future where the algorithmically identified subject is being offered a ticket for another movie. If, after seeing the ad, the subject buys the ticket, the marketing has been successful. The success of this ad tells less about the subject's own interests and more about the generative force of predictions and the ability to produce desires through the platform's functions. This is not so much a question of indoctrination at the level of thought as it is what Chun has outlined as manipulation of the regimes of the habitual.[34] For Chun, habit manifests in the idea of updating one's social media presence. To use social media is to be subjected to an endless process of repetition, which shelters us from what is novel and disruptive.[35] While the ad for that particular movie you were really hoping to see, shown on your social media feed, may be a happy accident, the fact that movie tickets were advertised to you hardly is. Rather than accidental, it is based on the online consumption habits of the masses. "Habit," as Chun argues, "is key to determining probabilities, for habits render past contingent repetitions into anticipatable connections."[36] Through the generation and exploitation of habit, the possible becomes realized, and the platform is capable of affecting us, creating subjects with particular needs and making things happen.

They Make Money from Your Data; Why Shouldn't You?

The management of the possible is where social media's big investments lie. The possible, according to Gilles Deleuze, is an "image of the real, while the real is supposed to resemble the possible."[37] This means that when social media sites operate with possible futures, when they are trying to anticipate what happens, they establish particular conditions under which only particular things can happen. In this model, the uncertainties, the unpredictabilities, do not exist as such; but they are performative in the sense that they produce what they name.[38] If the possible is the image of the real, everything is already predetermined, or at least conditioned—all our choices, actions, futures. What arises from these sometimes dystopian views of loss of autonomy and control is the question of privacy, resistance, and opting out of social media; if my life and the surrounding world become entangled with social media, do I even have the possibility to disconnect?

Opting out, as José van Dijck puts it, demands vigilance and awareness on at least two levels: how the platforms and businesses operate and how social media have shaped our understanding of the social.[39] In our world dominated by social media and encompassed by digital networks, what is important to recognize is that disconnection is real. Disconnection is always present in connections, but sometimes it is imperceptible. As such, it resembles how Deleuze in *Difference and Repetition* defines difference as a differential relation. He draws on Leibniz and how, in the 1700s, he was interested in the infinitesimal calculus as a value approaching zero.[40] This value, however, is so small that it cannot be perceived or measured. This definition, as Luciana Parisi explains, is based on the "Law of Continuity, according to which changes in nature are continuous" and there are no gaps.[41] It is a question of finding the infinitely small difference that escapes the senses but yet is present as a point of variation. According to Deleuze, "dx is minimal in relation to x, as dy is in relation to y, but that dy/dx is the internal qualitative relation, expressing the universal function independently of its particular numerical values."[42] As Daniel Smith notes, in the differential relation dx/dy, dy in relation to y is equal to zero, and dx in relation to x is equal to zero, because they are infinitely small quantities.[43] "Yet the relation 0/0 is not equal to zero, in the differential relation, the relation subsists even when the terms disappear," Smith finds.[44] In differential relation, the relation persists as a potentiality even if its terms have disappeared.

If we take this idea of the persistence of difference and use it to analyze the concept of disconnection itself, we see that when two disconnected things are joined together, the individual parts may disappear, but disconnection still exists as a potentiality. Being that is connected, to something, somehow, someway, somewhere, then, is always already disconnected at the level of potential, and disconnection simultaneously produces the limits for that connection.

By examining disconnections in different forms, this book has focused on the forces of engagement that capture and modulate social media users. Since the discussion of disconnections has been framed through Deleuze's difference, one could argue that the affirmative and positive side of disconnection as the potential for resistance and for something new to emerge has not gained as much attention as it perhaps deserves. Deleuze's concept of difference, as the contemporary discussion goes, is, after all, a concept of connectivism and productivism, fundamentally positive and not negative.[45]

This more affirmative side of disconnection, disconnection as creation, has been present in this book empirically in the context of art, which shows alternative ways to connect. These alternative ways are theoretically grounded in the concept of affect, which cannot be contained and captured entirely. Yet affect and art are not alternatives to connectivity but modes of interference. As Deleuze notes, "it is at the level of interference of many practices that things happen, beings, images, concepts, all the kinds of events."[46] Disconnections are modes of interference. Disconnections interrupt different flows, where "flow" is the expression of stimulus, response, or habit. Interruption produces a critical distance and awareness not by self-conscious thought but by the violence of interruption. Disconnection by interfering "enables a different connectivity, a different difference, in parallel," as Brian Massumi has argued.[47]

This interference is manifested in a project called Commodify.Us, which, through disconnection, tries to reveal how tightly social media are tied into the processes of mining and monetizing user data.[48] "They make money from your data. Why shouldn't you?" is the tagline of Commodify.Us, which identifies itself as "an internet startup which produces projects to help individuals capitalize on their online monetary potential."[49] Commodify.Us does not demand that the user leave the platform; rather, it asks for a disconnection at the level of data. First, Commodify.Us asks the user to download her data from Facebook. Then it provides a platform where the user uploads her social media data and analyzes their market value. The data are anonymized and the market value is based on social media engagement translated into social media metrics, such as a total number of words on a user's wall, the number of the user's friends, the user's account activity, and the number of pages the user admins. As the creators of the project note, "this is how you look to potential licensors of your data and likewise, to the people who run the social media websites."[50] After the market value of the user's social media engagement is evaluated, the user can choose to license the data and either keep them private, make them open to anyone, or choose a commercial data license and let Commodify.Us sell the user data to interested buyers. Commodify.Us lets "users manage, regulate, repattern and reappropriate their own data using tools that share an essential functionality (if not purpose) with the power tools of Web 2.0."[51]

Following Chun, to understand the modes of resistance against the intrusiveness of online networks, and social media, in this case, we should not stick to and defend our old notions of privacy but rather build on new modes of publicity.[52] Commodify.Us tries to give us a way to operate with the so-called private more publicly. With Commodify.Us, the awareness of our privacy being transformed into goods by social media businesses leads to very specific actions where the user is reappropriated by her own data for her own use, however rational or irrational the user may be. The project does not escape capitalism but tries to exploit it by interfering and repurposing its own logic. The question, then, is, does it give us a real alternative?

While leaving the question up in the air, I want to point out that even if disconnections are immanent to connections, they do not necessarily affirm anything positive. The alternative, the potential or the virtual, should not automatically be associated with the positive without hesitation. Making new connections should not be an end in itself. In fact, Andrew Culp has justly criticized the connectivist and productivist reading of Deleuze's difference, which leads into metaphysics of positivity, as naive.[53] The naivety of these connectivist and productivist readings comes from believing that reproducing the conditions of the present through new connections is the creation and offers the potential for something genuinely new to emerge.[54] Culp asks for a different reading of difference, not as a creation of something new, but simply as the destruction of this world, "the world of webs of connections, such as rhizomes, assemblages, networks, material systems, or dispositifs," which conditions have become intolerable.[55]

Epilogue: What's on Your Mind?

In the beginning and in the end, there was a distraction. The press named social media as a source of distraction that isolated people from their environments and made them neglect offline relationships at the expense of the online. But perhaps, ironically, according to Regina Dungan, the head of Facebook's innovation skunkworks Building 8, this addictive and distractive entity, which "allowed us to connect with people far away from us too often at the expense of people sitting right next to us," was in fact not social media but the smartphone.[56] The smartphone was this medium, manifested in its very material existence, that forced us to look down and not around us. Importantly, the smartphone, according to Dungan, was not negatively affecting social relationships but merely making users isolate themselves from the immediate unmediated surroundings.[57] What we did with the phone, such as writing status updates or posting photos on our social media sites, seemed to be trivial to the problem of distraction.

To solve the problem of distraction, Facebook wants to get rid of the physical device and replace it with a different interface to the platform. Indeed, what Facebook is planning next is already manifesting in its hiring plans for a brain–computer interface engineer: "We are looking for a slightly impatient individual willing to face down their fear of failure to accomplish bold things."[58] For Facebook, the distractions the smartphone causes can be solved by a system that interfaces directly with the brain. While a brain–computer interface of social media sounds like something out of Superman's rogues gallery, we should not be worried, Dungan convinces us: "This isn't about decoding random thoughts. This is about decoding the words you've already decided to share by sending them to the speech center of your brain."[59] To build this interface, Facebook is teaming up with different research institutions and looking into machine learning, neural prosthetics, and neuroimaging systems: "Even with its device, Facebook says you'll be able to think freely but only turn some thoughts into text."[60]

This development, if we follow Friedrich Kittler, is in line with the traditional history of communication media framed by thinkers such as Marshall McLuhan or Sigmund Freud through the human perspective; here media are seen as technical prosthetics, the externalization of first human sensory-motor capabilities and then human intelligence into a media interface.[61] But Kittler also gives us a different variation of the same history, where the human with their capabilities is not the primus motor of the developments of our media technologies; rather, the history of media is seen as a series of strategic escalations and interferences of and by the technology itself.[62]

For the nonhuman studies of social media, the moment of brain–computer interface denotes a more fundamental moment of capture where the human is fully absorbed into the network and the humanity of that node merely becomes its biotechnical feature. This is not, the cynic might say, unlike the derivative role given to us by the affective capitalism of targeted marketing and data analytics.

While interfacing social media directly with the brain could be contextualized as a technical invention, merely as a form of text generation not much different than typing with one's fingers, it is also part of a larger tendency in neuroculture and neuropower.[63] The brain–computer interface may give the user a new way to control her social media, but simultaneously, the user is subjected to new forms of control that tap into the brain and its functions. "What's on your mind?"

becomes a rhetorical question when a user's brainwaves could give the answer before a clear thought has been elaborated.

What's on your mind is indubitably also an issue that touches upon the idea of disconnecting quite literally, at least if we move from typing with brainwaves into controlling things like logging in or out from our social media profiles with our brains. In other words, if thinking becomes the way to control your Facebook profile, then thinking about disconnecting becomes the unthinkable in thought. Disconnection is pushed to the plane of immanence, which Gilles Deleuze and Félix Guattari describe as that which cannot be thought and that which must be thought at the same time: "It is the most intimate within thought and yet the absolute outside—an outside more distant than any external world because it is an inside deeper that any internal world."[64] Disconnection is the unthinkable, which we cannot not think if we want to be able to affect the present conditions and create the possibilities for something else. The more disconnection is pushed into the role of the infinitesimal, the smallest degree of intensity there is, the more important it is not only to think what disconnection is but to show that it is there, paraphrasing Deleuze and Guattari, as the possibility of the impossible.[65] For, if the distance between connection and disconnection is measured with the infinitesimal, it seems that sometimes the same could be said about the distances between human, nonhuman, and inhuman.

Acknowledgments

I would like to express my gratitude to a number of individuals and institutions for their irreplaceable support in helping me navigate through different stages of this work. This book would be very different without the excellent advice and support from my mentors Jussi Parikka and Jukka Sihvonen—when I asked questions, they had answers; when I thought I had answers, they had questions. I am also very grateful for the comprehensive feedback and encouragement I have received from Susanna Paasonen, Richard Grusin, Mark Coté, and Roy Roussel. Furthermore, I thank the University of Minnesota Press, in particular Doug Armato, Erin Warholm-Wohlenhaus, and Gabriel Levin. Much gratitude goes also to the anonymous reviewers.

I thank Kate Crawford for mentorship and Teri Rueb, Olli Sotamaa, and Nancy Baym for guidance and input in different stages of this path. To Mari Pajala, Ilona Hongisto, Marc Böhlen, Jukka-Pekka Puro, and Tommi Römpötti, your collegiality always made my work much easier. I have had the privilege to discuss this work with Taina Bucher, Mona Mannevuo, Tony D. Sampson, Pasi Väliaho, Mary Gray, Jessa Lingel, Olli Pyyhtinen, Alessandro Delfanti, Greg Elmer, Ganaele Langlois, Tanja Sihvonen, Jade Davis, Jacob Gallagher-Ross, Heikki Kinnari, Varpu Rantala, Andrew Herman, Veli-Matti Karhulahti, Outi Hakola, Satu Kyösola, Michaela Bränn, Jukka Kortti, Maiju Kannisto, Henri Weijo, Jaakko Nousiainen, Derek Curry, Ben Light, and Anne Kaun, among others.

This work has been funded with grants and awards by Elomedia, the Kone Foundation, the Turku University Foundation, Turun

Suomalainen Yliopistoseura, and the Emil Aaltonen Foundation. University of Turku, University at Buffalo, and University of Toronto provided me institutional support in many ways. I thank Holly Monteith, Jason Grice, and Martin Brink for their editing services. Kudos to Simo Arvo, Timo Keippilä, Miska Koivumäki, Teemu Toivola, Jussi Kaisjoki, Ria Vaahto, Hannamari Hoikkala, Josi Tikkanen, and Lasse Saarinen.

I thank Piritta and Atte Haarala and especially my parents, Pirkko and Hannu Karppi, whose support has been of vital importance. Finally, my deepest gratitude goes to Elina Tulla, who makes everything possible.

Notes

Log In

1. Mark Zuckerberg, "I believe the most important thing we can do is work to bring people closer together," Facebook status update, June 22, 2017, https://www.facebook.com/photo.php?fbid=10103818114983761.

2. Facebook Inc., "Form S-1: Registration Statement under the Securities Act of 1993," February 1, 2012, 67, https://www.sec.gov/Archives/edgar/data/1326801/000119312512034517/d287954ds1.htm#toc287954_10.

3. Andrew Culp, *Dark Deleuze* (Minneapolis: University of Minnesota Press, 2016), 12.

4. Ben Light, *Disconnecting with Social Networking Sites* (Basingstoke, U.K.: Palgrave Macmillan, 2014), 159.

5. Gilles Deleuze and Félix Guattari, "Gilles Deleuze and Félix Guattari on Anti-Oedipus," in *Negotiations, 1972–1990,* ed. Gilles Deleuze (New York: Columbia University Press, 1990), 21–22.

6. Gilles Deleuze, in *Difference and Repetition* (London: Continuum, 2004), 237, points out that these are the questions that let us focus on accidents, events, difference, and multiplicity. They are different questions than those asked when the focus is on the essence of things.

7. Tiziana Terranova, *Network Culture: Politics for the Information Age* (London: Pluto Books, 2004), 1.

8. In *Difference and Repetition*, Deleuze notes that "thought is primarily trespass and violence, the enemy, and nothing presupposes philosophy: everything begins with misosophy. Don't count upon thought to ensure the relative necessity of what it thinks. Rather, count upon the contingency of an encounter with that which forces thought to raise up and educate the absolute necessity of an act of thought or a passion to think. The conditions of true

critique and true creation are the same: the destruction of image of thought which presupposes itself and the genesis of the act of thinking in thought itself" (175–76).

9. Nathalie Casemajor, Stéphane Couture, Mauricio Delfin, Matthew Goerzen, and Alessandro Delfanti, in "Non-participation in Digital Media: Toward a Framework of Mediated Political Action," *Media, Culture, and Society* 37, no. 6 (2015): 860–63, have argued that we should divide the categories of participation and nonparticipation into passive and active modes. For example, passive nonparticipation indicates "unwillingness to participate due to economic, technical, physical, or social conditions" (860), whereas active nonparticipation "manifests in willful engagements aimed at slowing down, disrupting, or exiting platforms" (863). If we follow this categorization, active nonparticipation in specific builds on the understanding of disconnection.

10. Light, *Disconnecting with Social Networking Sites,* 155.

11. Light, 4.

12. Amanda Lagerkvist, "Existential Media: Toward a Theorization of Digital Thrownness," *New Media and Society,* Online First (June 7, 2016): 12.

13. Matt Haber, "A Trip to Camp to Break a Tech Addiction," *New York Times,* July 5, 2013, http://www.nytimes.com/2013/07/07/fashion/a-trip-to-camp-to-break-a-tech-addiction.html.

14. Haber.

15. Haber.

16. Amrita Deb, "Phantom Vibration and Phantom Ringing among Mobile Phone Users: A Systematic Review of Literature," *Asia-Pacific Psychiatry* 7, no. 3 (2015): 231.

17. Mark Deuze, "Media Life," *Media, Culture, and Society* 33, no. 1 (2011): 143.

18. Tony Sampson, "Various Joyful Encounters with the Dystopias of Affective Capitalism," *ephemera: theory and politics in organisation* 16, no. 4 (2016): 68.

19. Sampson, 70, 58.

20. Cal Newport, "Quit Social Media: Your Career May Depend on It," *New York Times,* November 19, 2016, http://www.nytimes.com/2016/11/20/jobs/quit-social-media-your-career-may-depend-on-it.html?_r=0.

21. See, e.g., Daniel J. Levitin, "Why the Modern World Is Bad for Your Brain," *Guardian,* January 18, 2015, https://www.theguardian.com/science/2015/jan/18/modern-world-bad-for-brain-daniel-j-levitin-organized-mind-information-overload; Daniel J. Leviting, "Hit the Reset Button in Your Brain," *New York Times,* August 9, 2014, accessed December 20, 2016, https://www.nytimes.com/2014/08/10/opinion/sunday/hit-the-reset-button-in-your-brain.html.

22. Laura Portwood-Stacer, "Media Refusal and Conspicuous Non-consumption: The Performative and Political Dimensions of Facebook Abstention," *New Media and Society* 15, no. 7 (2012): 1054.

23. José van Dijck, *The Culture of Connectivity: A Critical History of Social Media* (Oxford: Oxford University Press, 2013), 6–7.

24. Ryan Paul, "Jaiku Users Flee to Twitter as a Result of Google's Neglect (updated)," *ARSTechnica*, January 8, 2008, http://arstechnica.com/business /2008/01/jaiku-users-flee-to-twitter-as-a-result-of-googles-neglect/.

25. Bradley Horowitz, "A Fall Sweep," *Google Official Blog*, October 14, 2011, https://googleblog.blogspot.com/2011/10/fall-sweep.html.

26. Facebook Inc., "Form 10-K: Annual Report Pursuant to Section 13 or 15(d) of the Securities Exchange Act of 1934," January 28, 2016, 9.

27. Ben Light and Elijah Cassidy, "Strategies for the Suspension and Prevention of Connection: Rendering Disconnection as Socioeconomic Lubricant with Facebook," *New Media and Society* 16, no. 7 (2014): 1180.

28. Wendy Hui Kyong Chun, *Updating to Remain the Same: Habitual New Media* (Cambridge, Mass.: MIT Press, 2016), 69.

29. José Van Dijck, "Facebook and the Engineering of Connectivity: A Multi-layered Approach to Social Media Platforms," *Convergence* 19, no. 2 (2013): 141–55.

30. Taina Bucher, "The Friendship Assemblage: Investigating Programmed Sociality on Facebook," *Television and New Media,* Online First (August 24, 2012): 2.

31. Grant Bollmer, *Inhuman Networks: Social Media and the Archaeology of Connection* (New York: Bloomsbury, 2016), 5.

32. Gilles Deleuze, "Postscript on the Societies of Control," *October 59* (Winter 1992): 5.

33. Tony D. Sampson, *Virality: Contagion Theory in the Age of Networks* (Minneapolis: University of Minnesota Press, 2012), 159.

34. While I here use the singular *they* as a pronoun to speak about the social media user, in the following passages, I will use the gendered nouns. Gender for social media sites like Facebook or search engines like Google is one category used for tailoring content and targeting advertisements. The ways in which gender is assumed are heterogeneous; sometimes one is asked to provide this information when setting up their profile, other times the gender is being predicted based on users' browsing habits, for example. The assumed gender may well differ from the gender one identifies with, but even if erroneous, for the platform, it is a category meant to make sense. Hence, when I use gendered nouns, I am not making gender assumptions per se; rather, I want to note how each user is already gendered through their social media engagements. See John Cheney-Lippold, "A New Algorithmic Identity: Soft

Biopolitics and the Modulation of Control," *Theory, Culture, and Society* 28, no. 6 (2011): 164–81.

35. Mark Hansen, "Media Theory," *Theory, Culture, and Society* 23, no. 2–3 (2006): 2.

36. On the emergence of the notion of the nonhuman turn and its different approaches, see Richard Grusin, introduction to *The Non-human Turn,* ed. Richard Grusin (Minneapolis: University of Minnesota Press, 2015).

37. Friedrich Kittler, "The History of Communication Media," *CTheory* 114 (July 30, 1996); Friedrich Kittler, *Optical Media* (Cambridge: Polity, 2010), 36.

38. Geoffrey Winthrop-Young, *Kittler and the Media* (Cambridge: Polity, 2011), 65.

39. See Mark Hansen, *Embodying Technesis: Technology beyond Writing* (Ann Arbor: University of Michigan Press, 2003), 225.

40. Friedrich A. Kittler, *Gramophone, Film, Typewriter* (Stanford, Calif.: Stanford University Press, 1999), xl.

41. Deleuze, *Difference and Repetition,* 176.

42. Deleuze, 175–76.

43. Matthew Fuller, "Introduction: The Stuff of Software," in *Software Studies: A Lexicon* (Cambridge, Mass.: MIT Press, 2008), 4.

44. Wendy Hui Kyong Chun, *Programmed Visions: Software and Memory* (Cambridge, Mass.: MIT Press, 2011), 66–67.

45. Alexander Galloway, *The Interface Effect* (Cambridge: Polity, 2012), 69. Emphasis in the original text.

46. Carolin Gerlitz, "What Counts? Reflections on the Multivalence of Social Media Data," *Digital Culture and Society* 2, no. 2 (2016): 20.

47. Tarleton Gillespie, "Regulation of and by Platforms," in *Sage Handbook of Social Media,* ed. Jean Burgess, Thomas Poell, and Alice Marwick (Thousand Oaks, Calif.: Sage, forthcoming).

48. Cf. Bernhard Siegert, *Cultural Techniques: Grids, Filters, Doors, and Other Articulations of the Real* (New York: Fordham University Press, 2015).

49. See Sampson, *Virality*; Chun, *Updating to Remain the Same.*

50. Cf. Anna Munster, *An Aesthesia of Networks: Conjunctive Experience in Art and Technology* (Cambridge, Mass.: MIT Press, 2013), 7.

51. See Jussi Parikka, "Archival Media Theory: An Introduction to Wolfgang Ernst's Media Archaeology," in *Digital Memory and the Archive,* by Wolfgang Ernst, ed. Jussi Parikka (Minneapolis: University of Minnesota Press, 2013), 11.

52. Cf. Juliette Garside, "Facebook Will Lose 80% of Users by 2017, Say Princeton Researchers," *Guardian,* January 22, 2014, http://www.theguardian.com/technology/2014/jan/22/facebook-princeton-researchers-infectious-disease.

53. Facebook Inc., "Form S-1," 11.

54. David Goldman, "Twitter Is Losing Customers and Its Stock Is Falling," CNN Money, February 10, 2016, http://money.cnn.com/2016/02/10/technology/twitter-stock-users/.

55. David Beer, *Metric Power* (London: Palgrave Macmillan, 2016), 151.

56. See also Sampson, *Virality*, 32.

57. Yuval Dror, "'We Are Not Here for the Money': Founders' manifestos," *New Media and Society* 17, no. 4 (2015): 546–47.

58. Facebook Inc., "Form S-1," 67.

59. Facebook Inc., 67.

60. Twitter, "Form S-1: Registration Statement under the Securities Act of 1993," October 3, 2013, 91, https://www.sec.gov/Archives/edgar/data/1418091/000119312513390321/d564001ds1.htm.

61. Beverley Skeggs and Simon Yuill, "Capital Experimentation with Person/a Formation: How Facebook's Monetization Refigures the Relationship between Property, Personhood and Protest," *Information, Communication, and Society* 19, no. 3 (2016): 384–86.

62. Facebook Inc., *Annual Report 2015* (Menlo Park, Calif.: Facebook Inc., 2015), 5.

63. Twitter Inc., *Annual Report 2016* (San Francisco, Calif: Twitter Inc., 2015), 5.

64. Steven Shaviro, *Connected or What it Means to Live in a Networked Society*, (Minneapolis: University of Minnesota Press, 2003), 4.

65. Helen Kennedy and Giles Moss, "Known or Knowing Publics? Social Media Data Mining and the Question of Public Agency," *Big Data and Society*, July–December 2015, 2–4.

66. Michel Foucault, "Truth and Power," in *Power/Knowledge: Selected Interviews and Other Writings 1927–1977*, ed. Colin Gordon (New York: Pantheon Books, 1980), 119.

67. In Foucault's writings, power is, first of all, productive. Power produces, regulates, distributes, and circulates. It produces knowledge, discourses, and new practices. Second, power is not centrally controlled but takes place in relations between people, societies, infrastructures, and architectures.

68. Ganaele Langlois, *Meaning in the Age of Social Media* (New York: Palgrave Macmillan, 2014), 171–72.

69. danah boyd and Kate Crawford, "Critical Questions for Big Data," *Information, Communication, and Society* 15, no. 5 (2012): 662–79.

70. Nancy K. Baym, "Data Not Seen: The Uses and Shortcomings of Social Media Metrics," *First Monday* 18, no. 10 (2013), http://firstmonday.org/article/view/4873/3752.

71. Van Dijck, *Culture of Connectivity*, 4.

72. Van Dijck, 13.

73. Van Dijck, 4.

74. Mark Zuckerberg, "I want to share some thoughts on Facebook and the election," Facebook status update, November 12, 2016, accessed December 19, 2016, https://www.facebook.com/zuck/posts/10103253901916271.

75. Facebook user, November 12, 2016, comment on Zuckerberg, "I want to share some thoughts."

76. Zuckerberg, "I want to share some thoughts."

77. Zuckerberg.

78. The notion of "nonhuman" in this context refers to the philosophical and political discussions that challenge the idea of matter being passive, raw, or, for example, given and instead try to see matter as a vibrant agency with a capability to affect and be affected. In these discussions, matter matters in itself, not only as a part of a social system or other embodied human perspective. See Jane Bennett, *Vibrant Matter: A Political Ecology of Things* (Durham, N.C.: Duke University Press, 2010). In addition, it is noted that there are also other users than the human user operating on Facebook and social media sites. Artificial agents, such as bots, have the capability to conduct humanlike operations and interactions and blur the lines between different users. See Nikolaos Mavridis, "Artificial Agents Entering Social Networks," in *A Networked Self: Identity, Community, and Culture on Social Network Sites,* ed. Zizi Papacharissi, 291–303 (New York: Routledge, 2011).

79. McKenzie Funk, "The Secret Agenda of a Facebook Quiz," *New York Times,* November 19, 2016, http://www.nytimes.com/2016/11/20/opinion/the-secret-agenda-of-a-facebook-quiz.html.

80. Cambridge Analytica, https://cambridgeanalytica.org/about.

81. Funk, "Secret Agenda of a Facebook Quiz."

82. On March 17, 2018, three days after this book had gone into production, *The New York Times, The Observer,* and *The Guardian* launched a series of news stories describing in detail how Cambridge Analytica had acquired data from 50 million Facebook users in order to build psychographic models that could be used for targeting advertisements. This news drew instant responses not only from lawmakers and the scientific community demanding better regulation of Facebook data but also from social media users themselves. The issues of deleting one's Facebook and leaving the site were brought to the front once again. The hashtag #DeleteFacebook became a symbol of this resistance. Time will tell what the actual effects of these revelations are. However, even a quick look at the event corroborates what is highlighted in this book: disconnection is an economic threat to Facebook and rather than destructive, it is productive. Financial reporters argued that the week following the Cambridge Analytica revelations was the worst week for the Facebook stock since 2012. Mark Zuckerberg took action posting an ad in

several newspapers explaining the reasons for the data breach and explaining how they would respond and change their practices. "I promise to do better for you," Zuckerberg ended his ad addressing the Facebook community. Disconnection became an opening to think about our social media engagements not only for individual social media users but also for the company itself. This, of course, if you follow the arguments made in this book, is not new. What has been new in the discussions is the observation that not everyone can quit. This implicates that the tactics of expansion and the projects to intensify user engagement, which I discuss in detail in chapters 1 and 5, have been indeed successful and #DeleteFacebook has become an option hardly anyone chooses.

83. Taina Bucher, "Want to Be on the Top? Algorithmic Power and the Threat of Invisibility on Facebook," *New Media and Society* 14, no. 7 (2012): 1164–80.

84. Scott Lash, "Power after Hegemony," *Theory, Culture, and Society* 24, no. 3 (2007): 71.

85. Bernhard Rieder, "What Is in PageRank? A Historical and Conceptual Investigation of a Recursive Status Index," *Computational Culture*, September 28, 2012.

86. Cf. Engin Bozdag, "Bias in Algorithmic Filtering and Personalization," *Ethics and Information Technology* 15, no. 3 (2013): 209.

87. See Michael T. Parker and Linda M. Isbell, "How I Vote Depends on How I Feel: The Differential Impact of Anger and Fear on Political Information Processing," *Psychological Science* 21, no. 4 (2010): 549.

88. R. Kelly Garrett, "Facebook's Problem Is More Complicated Than Fake News," *The Conversation*, November 16, 2016, https://theconversation.com/facebooks-problem-is-more-complicated-than-fake-news-68886.

89. Adam D. I. Kramer, Jamie E. Guillory, and Jeffrey T. Hancock, "Experimental Evidence of Massive-Scale Emotional Contagion through Social Networks," *Proceedings of the National Academy of Sciences of the United States of America* 111, no. 24 (2014): 8788.

90. Kramer et al., 8789.

91. Tony D. Sampson, *The Assemblage Brain: Sense Making in Neuroculture* (Minneapolis: University of Minnesota Press, 2016), 99–100.

92. Susanna Paasonen, Ken Hillis, and Michael Petit, "Introduction: Networks of Transmission: Intensity, Sensation, Value," in *Networked Affect*, ed. Ken Hillis, Susanna Paasonen, and Michael Petit (Cambridge, Mass.: MIT Press, 2015), 10.

93. Paasonen et al., 7.

94. Brian Massumi, *Parables for the Virtual: Movement, Affect, Sensation* (Durham, N.C.: Duke University Press, 2002), 32.

95. Sampson, *Assemblage Brain*, 19–20.

96. Richard Grusin, "Radical Mediation," *Critical Inquiry* 42, no. 1 (2015): 125.

97. Cf. Anne Kaun and Christian Schwarzenegger, "'No Media, Less Life?' Online Disconnection in Mediatized Worlds," *First Monday* 19, no. 11 (2014), http://www.firstmonday.org/ojs/index.php/fm/article/view/5497/4158.

98. Van Dijck, "Facebook and the Engineering of Connectivity," 152.

99. The caveat of Facebook research is that social media platforms are, as Nicole B. Ellison and Danah M. Boyd in "Sociality through Social Network Sites," in *The Oxford Handbook of Internet Studies,* ed. William H. Dutton (Oxford: Oxford University Press, 2013), mention, in "perpetual beta." They change and transform constantly. Between 2010 and 2018, a lot has changed not only from a sociocultural perspective but also regarding the technological features of the platform. The News Feed has gone through visual and technical changes. Facebook introduced and stopped using features such as Ticker or Sponsored Stories. Policies, help desk information, and developer guidelines are being updated. Facebook's legal terms are being updated. While some of these changes are noted in this book, tracking all of them has not been the purpose of this study. Instead, I have tried to situate the materials in cultural and sociotechological contexts that express the relationality of Facebook's affective bonds.

100. Brian Massumi, *Politics of Affect* (Cambridge: Polity, 2015), 205.

101. Massumi, 205, 215.

102. Deleuze, "Postscript on the Societies of Control," 4.

103. Michel Foucault, *"The Archaeology of Knowledge" and "The Discourse on Language"* (New York: Pantheon Books, 1972), 4, 5, 14.

104. Deleuze, *Difference and Repetition.*

105. Cliff Stagoll, "Difference," in *The Deleuze Dictionary,* ed. Adrian Parr (New York: Columbia University Press, 2005), 73.

106. Deleuze, *Difference and Repetition,* 330. Even deconstructing the etymology of *disconnect* shows that disconnection is an issue of difference, not by comparison between two terms that have individual identities but as a force capable of producing an identity as such. The root, *connect,* is based on a Latin verb *connectere,* which has two parts: *con-* (together) + *nectere* (bind). *To connect* is "to join together, unite physically." The prefix *dis-* (primary meaning in Latin of "two ways, in twain") indicates a differential relation where separation of the two parts exists as a potentiality. Disconnection, then, is not to be understood as different to connection (not-connection) but rather always belongs to a connection.

107. Light, *Disconnecting with Social Networking Sites,* 159.

108. Paul Virilio, "The Primal Accident," in *The Politics of Everyday Fear,* ed. Brian Massumi (Minneapolis: University of Minnesota Press, 1993), 212.

109. Gilles Deleuze and Félix Guattari, *A Thousand Plateaus: Capitalism and Schizophrenia* (Minneapolis: University of Minnesota Press, 2005), 376–77.

Engage

1. Katie Hope, "Facebook Now Used by Half of World's Online Users," BBC News, July 29, 2015, http://www.bbc.com/news/business-33712729.

2. Nicholas Carlson, "MySpace Passed on Buying Facebook for $75 Million," *Business Insider,* January 26, 2009, http://www.businessinsider.com /2009/1/myspace-passed-on-buying-facebook-for-75-million.

3. Robert W. Gehl, "Real (Software) Abstractions: On the Rise of Facebook and the Fall of MySpace," *Social Text 111* 30, no. 2 (2012): 100.

4. Facebook Inc., "Form 10-K," in *Annual Report 2015,* 8.

5. Michel Foucault, *Security, Territory, Population: Lectures at the Collège de France 1977–1978* (New York: Palgrave Macmillan, 2009).

6. Tiziana Terranova, "Securing the Social: Foucault and Social Networks," in *Foucault and the History of the Present,* ed. Sophie Fuggle, Yari Lanci, and Martina Tazzioli (New York: Palgrave Macmillan, 2015), 112–13.

7. Michel Foucault, *Discipline and Punish* (New York: Pantheon Books, 1977).

8. Taina Bucher, "Want to Be on the Top? Algorithmic Power and the Threat of Invisibility on Facebook," *New Media and Society* 14, no. 7 (2012): 7.

9. Foucault, *Discipline and Punish,* 201.

10. Foucault, *Security, Territory, Population,* 29.

11. Terranova, "Securing the Social," 114.

12. Foucault, *Security, Territory, Population,* 20–21.

13. Foucault, 96; on Facebook becoming ubiquitous, see Portwood-Stacer, "Media Refusal and Conspicuous Non-consumption," 1047, and chapter 6.

14. Terranova, "Securing the Social," 112, 124.

15. Terranova, 124–25.

16. Foucault, *Security, Territory, Population,* 21.

17. Ulises A. Mejias, "The Limits of Networks as Models for Organizing the Social," *New Media and Society* 12, no. 4 (2010): 603–17.

18. Mejias, 614.

19. Facebook Inc., *Annual Report 2015,* 8–9.

20. See Ben Light and Elija Cassidy, "Strategies for the Suspension and

Prevention of Connection: Rendering Disconnection as Socioeconomic Lubricant with Facebook," *New Media and Society* 16, no. 7 (2014): 1171, where the authors correspondingly argue that disconnection not only challenges Facebook but can also work as a way to secure its existence. See also chapter 5.

21. Facebook Inc., *Annual Report 2015,* 8.

22. Henry Jenkins, Sam Ford, and Joshua Green, *Spreadable Media: Creating Value and Meaning in a Networked Culture* (New York: New York University Press, 2013), 116.

23. Henry Jenkins interviewed by Frank Rose, "Henry Jenkins on 'Spreadable Media': How Web 2.0 Went Wrong, Why 'Viral' Sucks, and the UGC Problem," *Deep Media,* January 22, 2013.

24. Jenkins et al., *Spreadable Media,* 56–57.

25. I am strongly associating users here with the definition of bodies in the context of affect theory; bodies that affect are always simultaneously affected. Participation is not possible without engagement, which operates on the levels of affect. Affect here is transindividual. Affect triggers a response. I return to the problem of affect later in this chapter.

26. Jenkins et al., *Spreadable Media,* 3–4.

27. Facebook Inc., "Form S-1."

28. Facebook, "How to Target Ads," accessed September 29, 2016, https://www.facebook.com/business/a/online-sales/ad-targeting-details.

29. Facebook.

30. Facebook.

31. Mark Zuckerberg, "F8 Keynote," September 22, 2011, https://f8.facebook.com.

32. Irina Kaldrack and Theo Röhle, "Divide and Share: Taxonomies, Orders and Masses in Facebook's Open Graph," *Computational Culture: A Journal of Software Studies* 4 (2014), http://www.computationalculture.net/. See also chapter 2 in this book.

33. Robert Payne, "Frictionless Sharing and Digital Promiscuity," *Communication and Critical/Cultural Studies,* January 30, 2014, 5.

34. Payne. See also chapter 2.

35. Payne, 5.

36. Molly Wood, quoted in Payne, 5.

37. Payne, 5–6.

38. Cf. Terranova, "Securing the Social," 114.

39. Carolin Gerlitz and Anne Helmond, "The Like Economy: Social Buttons and the Data Intensive Web," *New Media and Society* 15, no. 8 (2013): 1349.

40. Gerlitz and Helmond, 1349.

41. *Oxford Living Dictionaries,* s.v. "engage," https://en.oxforddictionaries.com/definition/engage.

42. *Oxford Living Dictionaries,* s.v. "gage," https://en.oxforddictionaries.com/definition/gage.

43. Massumi, *Parables for the Virtual,* 25.

44. Massumi.

45. Matthew Fuller, *Media Ecologies: Materialist Energies in Art and Technoculture* (Cambridge, Mass.: MIT Press, 2005), 172.

46. Brian Massumi, *The Power at the End of Economy* (Durham, N.C.: Duke University Press, 2014), 109.

47. Gilles Deleuze, "Postscript on the Societies of Control," *October* 59 (Winter 1992): 5.

48. Deleuze.

49. Kevin Haggerty and Richard Ericson, "The Surveillant Assemblage," *British Journal of Sociology* 51, no. 4 (2000): 616.

50. Facebook, "Lookalike Audiences," accessed September 29, 2016, https://www.facebook.com/business/a/lookalike-audiences.

51. Haggerty and Ericson, "Surveillant Assemblage," 614.

52. Massumi, *Power at the End of Economy,* 8–9.

53. Gabriel Tarde, "Economic Psychology," *Economy and Society* 36, no. 4 (2007): 631.

54. Massumi, *Power at the End of Economy,* 8.

55. Massumi, 9.

56. See also Terranova's "Securing the Social," 117–18, where she points out that Foucault, after analyzing neoliberalism, went back to eighteenth-century liberal thinkers to describe how a society is not built only on economic bonds; individuals in a society are also connected with more emotion-based bonds, such as "bonds of sympathy" and "bonds of repugnance."

57. Sampson, *Virality,* 20.

58. Tarde, "Economic Psychology," 631.

59. Massumi, *Power at the End of Economy,* 9.

60. Massumi, 8.

61. Tim O'Reilly, "What Is Web 2.0: Design Patterns and Business Models for the Next Generation of Software," *O'Reilly* (blog), September 30, 2005, http://www.oreilly.com/pub/a/web2/archive/what-is-web-20.html.

62. Anne Helmond, "The Platformization of the Web: Making Web Data Platform Ready," *Social Media + Society* 1, no. 2 (2015): 1–2.

63. Facebook, "Platform Is Here," June 2, 2007, https://www.facebook.com/notes/facebook/platform-is-here/2437282130.

64. Facebook, "Facebook Expands Power of Platform across the Web and

around the World," July 23, 2008, http://newsroom.fb.com/news/2008/07/ facebook-expands-power-of-platform-across-the-web-and-around-the-world/.

65. Helmond, "Platformization of the Web," 2.

66. Ganaele Langlois, "Participatory Culture and the New Governance of Communication: The Paradox of Participatory Media," *Television and New Media* 14, no. 2 (2013): 99–100.

67. Tim O'Reilly, "Web 2.0 Compact Definition: Trying Again," *O'Reilly Radar* (blog), December 10, 2006, http://radar.oreilly.com/2006/12/web-20 -compact-definition-tryi.html.

68. Facebook Inc., *Annual Report 2015*, 8–9.

69. Facebook Inc., "Form S-1."

70. Foucault, *Security, Territory, Population*, 29.

71. Foucault, 45.

72. Facebook Inc., *Annual Report 2015*, 9.

73. Facebook Inc.

74. Facebook, "Testing a New Way for People to Discover and Buy Products on Facebook," Facebook Business, July 17, 2014, https://www.facebook .com/business/news/Discover-and-Buy-Products-on-Facebook-Test.

75. Facebook, "Testing a New Way for People to Discover and Buy Products on Facebook."

76. Facebook, "How Do I Send or Receive Money in Messenger?," accessed December 19, 2016, https://www.facebook.com/help/messenger-app/ iphone/1386234371667067?rdrhc.

77. Georg Simmel, *Philosophy of Money* (New York: Routledge, 1900).

78. Joe DeVille, in *Lived Economies of Default: Consumer Credit, Debt Collection, and the Capture of Affect* (London: Routledge, 2015), 135, speaks specifically about credit cards, but similar arguments can be made about all payment cards, especially the ones tied to a credit card infrastructure.

79. José van Dijck, "Facebook and the Engineering of Connectivity: A Multi-layered Approach to Social Media Platforms," *Convergence* 19, no. 2 (2013): 141–55.

80. Sally Davies, Duncan Robinson, and Hannah Kuchler, "Facebook Targets Financial Services," *Financial Times,* April 13, 2014.

81. David Birch, "Forget Banks, in 2018 You'll Pay through Amazon and Facebook," *Wired,* January 2, 2018, http://www.wired.co.uk/article/ banks-data-tech-giants.

82. ATB Financial, "ATB First Full-Service FI in North America to Offer Chatbot Banking on Facebook Messenger," http://www.atb.com/about/news/ Pages/article.aspx?aid=616.

83. Reuters Staff, "Third of Global Consumers Open to Google, Amazon Banking: Survey," Reuters, January 11, 2017, https://www.reuters.com/article/

us-wealth-financialservices-survey/third-of-global-consumers-open-to-google
-amazon-banking-survey-idUSKBN14V2I2.

84. Davies et al.

85. Mark Zuckerberg, "The Hacker Way," CNN Money, February 1, 2012, http://money.cnn.com/2012/02/01/technology/zuckerberg_ipo_letter/.

86. Facebook, "Technology Leaders Launch Partnership to Make Internet Access Available to All," Facebook Newsroom, August 21, 2013, http://newsroom.fb.com/news/2013/08/technology-leaders-launch-partnership-to-make-internet-access-available-to-all.

87. Ahiza Garcia, "Mark Zuckerberg: Internet Access Can Eradicate Extreme Poverty," CNN Money, September 27, 2015, http://money.cnn.com/2015/09/26/news/mark-zuckerberg-united-nations-poverty-internet/.

88. These propositions echo the techno-optimist discourses of the 1990s, where the information superhighway, which we now simply call the internet, was seen as a liberator from the constraints of time, physical location, and economic inequality. In the United States, the overall connectivity was touted to provide solutions for the nation's education, regardless of the people's income levels. The internet, as we now know, came, but the educational problems remained unresolved. While Gore was driving the expansion of the internet on a national level in the 1990s, we now see that the same discourses are evoked in the global context.

89. See the website Internet.org, "Connecting the World from the Sky," March 28, 2014, https://info.internet.org/en/blog/2014/03/28/connecting-the-world-from-the-sky/; and see the eponymous document that, on the Internet.org site, is credited to Zuckerberg, "Connecting the World from the Sky," no date, https://info.internet.org/en/wp-content/uploads/sites/4/2016/07/851574_611544752265540_1262758947_n.pdf.

90. Zuckerberg, "Connecting the World from the Sky".

91. Mark Zuckerberg, Facebook post, March 27, 2014, https://www.facebook.com/zuck/posts/10101322049893211.

92. Mark Zuckerberg, "The Technology behind Aquila," July 21, 2016, https://www.facebook.com/notes/mark-zuckerberg/the-technology-behind-aquila/10153916136506634/.

93. Zuckerberg, "Connecting the World from the Sky."

94. Mark Zuckerberg, Facebook post, October 5, 2015, https://www.facebook.com/zuck/posts/10102407675865061.

95. Jussi Parikka, The Anthrobscene (Minneapolis: University of Minnesota Press, 2015).

96. Ed Malecki and Hu Wei, "A Wired World: The Evolving Geography of Submarine Cables and the Shift to Asia," Annals of the Association of American Geographers 99 (2009): 366.

97. Malecki and Wei.

98. Facebook for Developers, "Free Basics Platform," accessed December 19, 2016, https://developers.facebook.com/docs/internet-org.

99. Ariel Futter and Alison Gillwald, "Zero-Rated Internet Services: What Is to Be Done? (Policy Paper 1, ResearchICTAfrica.net, 2015), 3–4; Martin Moore, *Tech Giants and Civic Power* (London: Center for the Study of Media, Communications, and Power, Kings College London, 2015), 29.

100. Cf. Alfred North Whitehead, who, in *Process and Reality* (New York: Free Press, 1978), notes that propositions lure for feeling, and as such, they direct thought (184). They are termini-of-action, as Erin Manning, in "Creative Propositions for Thought in Motion," *Inflexions* 1, no. 1 (2008): 18, puts it.

Participate

1. Douglas Rushkoff, "Why I'm Quitting Facebook," CNN, February 25, 2013, http://www.cnn.com/2013/02/25/opinion/rushkoff-why-im-quitting -facebook.

2. Rushkoff.

3. Rushkoff.

4. Facebook, "Does Facebook Use My Name or Photo in Ads?," accessed May 23, 2017, https://www.facebook.com/help/214816128640041.

5. Light, *Disconnecting with Social Networking Sites,* 49.

6. Kaun and Schwarzenegger, "No Media, Less Life?"

7. Rushkoff, "Why I'm Quitting Facebook."

8. Facebook Inc., "Introducing Timeline," 2012, no longer available.

9. Samuel W. Lessin, "Tell Your Story with Timeline," *Facebook Blog,* September 22, 2011, https://www.facebook.com/notes/facebook/tell-your -story-with-timeline/10150289612087131/.

10. Lessin.

11. Brian Massumi, *The Principle of Unrest: Activist Philosophy in the Expanded Field* (London: Open Humanities Press, 2017), 29.

12. Cf. Tiziana Terranova, "Free Labor: Producing Culture for the Digital Economy," *Social Text* 18, no. 2 (2000): 38.

13. Light, *Disconnecting with Social Networking Sites,* 47.

14. Susanna Paasonen, *Carnal Resonance: Affect and Online Pornography* (Cambridge, Mass.: MIT Press, 2011), 258.

15. Wendy Hui Kyong Chun, *Control and Freedom: Power and Paranoia in the Age of Fiber Optics* (Cambridge, Mass.: MIT Press, 2006) 249.

16. Chun, 250.

17. Cf. Arnold Roosendal, "Facebook Tracks and Traces Everyone: Like

This!" (Legal Studies Research Paper Series, Tilburg Law School, Tilburg, Netherlands, 2011), 3.

18. Maurizio Lazzarato, "Immaterial Labor," in *Radical Thought in Italy: A Potential Politics,* ed. Paolo Virno and Michael Hardt (Minneapolis: University of Minnesota Press, 1996), 137.

19. Facebook Inc., "Form S-1."

20. Facebook Inc., 3.

21. Facebook Inc., 2.

22. Facebook Inc., 3.

23. Daniel Rosenberg and Anthony Grafton, *Cartographies of Time* (New York: Princeton Architectural Press, 2010), 20.

24. Rosenberg and Grafton, *Cartographies of Time,* 13.

25. Cf. Gilles Deleuze, *Foucault* (Minneapolis: University of Minnesota Press, 1988), 37.

26. Henry Jenkins, *Convergence Culture: Where New and Old Media Collide* (New York: New York University Press, 2006), 3.

27. Jenkins, passim.

28. Yochai Benkler, *The Wealth of Networks: How Social Production Transforms Markets and Freedom* (New Haven, Conn.: Yale University Press, 2006); Jenkins, *Convergence Culture;* Axel Bruns, *Blogs, Wikipedia, Second Life, and Beyond: From Production to Produsage* (New York: Peter Lang, 2008).

29. Benkler, *Wealth of Networks,* 2.

30. Bruns, *Blogs, Wikipedia, Second Life, and Beyond,* 387.

31. Mirko Tobias Schäfer, *Bastard Culture! How User Participation Transforms Cultural Production* (Amsterdam: Amsterdam University Press, 2011), 51.

32. Schäfer, 44, 78.

33. Schäfer, 51.

34. Terranova, *Network Culture,* 91–94.

35. Schäfer, *Bastard Culture,* 78.

36. José van Dijck, "Users Like You? Theorizing Agency in User-Generated Content," *Media, Culture, and Society* 31, no. 1 (2009): 47.

37. Gehl, "Real (Software) Abstractions," 100.

38. Rushkoff, "Why I'm Quitting Facebook."

39. Massumi, *Principle of Unrest,* 11–12, 29, 41.

40. Gerlitz and Helmond, "Like Economy," 1354.

41. See, e.g., van Dijck, "Users Like You?"

42. Ian Tucker, "Douglas Rushkoff: 'I'm Thinking It May Be Good to Be Off Social Media Altogether,'" *Guardian,* February 12, 2016, https://

www.theguardian.com/technology/2016/feb/12/digital-capitalism-douglas -rushkoff. The "Experimental Evidence of Massive-Scale Emotional Contagion" research project by Kramer et al., where the researchers tweaked the positive and negative posts on News Feed to cause emotional responses can also be seen as being part of this discussion. See also the introduction and chapter 5 of this volume.

43. Rushkoff, "Why I'm Quitting Facebook."

44. Massumi, *Parables for the Virtual,* 45.

45. Massumi, 45.

46. Mark Zuckerberg, "F8 Keynote." See a liveblog of the event by Alexia Tsotsis, "Live From Facebook's 2011 F8 Conference," TechCrunch September 22, 2011: https://techcrunch.com/2011/09/22/live-from-facebooks-2011 -f8-conference-video/.

47. Cf. Ganaele Langlois, Fenwick McKelvey, Greg Elmer, and Kenneth Werbin, "Mapping Commercial Web 2.0 Worlds: Towards a New Critical Ontogenesis," *Fibreculture,* no. 14 (2009), accessed October 24, 2016, http://fourteen.fibreculturejournal.org/fcj-095-mapping-commercial-web-2 -0-worlds-towards-a-new-critical-ontogenesis/; Taina Bucher, "Objects of Intense Feeling: The Case of the Twitter API," *Computational Culture,* no. 3 (November 2013), accessed October 24, 2016, http://computationalculture .net/article/objects-of-intense-feeling-the-case-of-the-twitter-api.

48. Cf. Alexander Galloway, *Protocol: How Control Exists after Decentralization* (Cambridge, Mass.: MIT Press, 2004), 243–44.

49. Helmond, "Platformization of the Web," 1.

50. Taina Bucher, "A Technicity of Attention: How Software Makes Sense," *Culture Machine* 13 (2012): 5.

51. Helmond, "Platformization of the Web," 7.

52. Jennifer van Grove, "The Washington Post Launches Social Reader as a Newspaper for Facebook," *Mashable,* September 22, 2011, https://mashable .com/2011/09/22/social-reader/#.gHxyyVqTmqL.

53. Irina Kaldrack and Theo Röhle, "Divide and Share: Taxonomies, Orders and Amasses in Facebook's Open Graph," *Computational Culture.* no. 4 (November 9, 2014), http://computationalculture.net/article/divide-and-share.

54. Robert Payne, "Frictionless Sharing and Digital Promiscuity," *Communication and Critical/Cultural Studies,* January 30, 2014, 3–4, 11.

55. Alexia Tsotsis, "Live from Facebook's 2011 F8 Conference," *TechCrunch,* September 22, 2011, https://techcrunch.com/2011/09/22/live-from -facebooks-2011-f8-conference-video/.

56. Paul Virilio, "The Primal Accident," in Massumi, *Politics of Everyday Fear,* 211–18.

57. Bucher, "A Technicity of Attention," 12, 14–15.

58. Sara Ahmed, "Happy Objects," in *The Affect Theory Reader,* ed. Melissa Gregg and Gregory J. Seigworth (Durham, N.C.: Duke University Press, 2010), 29.

59. Bucher, "A Technicity of Attention," 12.

60. Jennifer Pybus, "Affect and Subjectivity: A Case Study of Neopets.com," *Politics and Culture* 2007, no. 2 (2007), http://www.politicsandculture.org /2009/10/02/jennifer-pybus-affect-and-subjectivity-a-case-study-of-neopets -com/.

61. Pybus.

62. Skeggs and Wood, *Reacting to Reality Television. Performance, Audience and Value* (New York: Routledge, 2012), 5.

63. Pybus, "Affect and Subjectivity."

64. Gilles Deleuze, *Spinoza: Practical Philosophy* (San Francisco: City Lights Books, 1988).

65. Brian Massumi, interviewed by Mary Zournazi, http://www.inter national-festival.org/node/111.

66. Gabriel Tarde, "Economic Psychology," *Economy and Society* 36, no. 4 (2007): 614–43; See also Kaldrack and Röhle, "Divide and Share."

67. Bruno Latour and Vincent Antonin Lépinay, *The Science of Passionate Interests: An Introduction to Gabriel Tarde's Economic Anthropology* (Chicago: Prickly Paradigm Press, 2009), 8–10; see also Sampson, *Virality,* 164.

68. Galloway, *Protocol,* 7–8.

69. Bucher, "A Technicity of Attention," 8.

70. Facebook Developers, "Open Graph," accessed June 11, 2012, https:// developers.facebook.com/docs/opengraph.

71. Van Grove, "Washington Post Launches Social Reader."

72. Facebook Developers, "Open Graph."

73. Facebook Developers, "Open Graph: Key Concepts," https://developers .facebook.com/docs/opengraph/keyconcepts/.

74. Van Dijck, "Users Like You?," 46.

75. Bennett, *Vibrant Matter.*

76. Bennett, 21–22.

77. Deleuze and Guattari, *A Thousand Plateaus,* 257.

78. Bennet, *Vibrant Matter,* xii.

79. Douglas Rushkoff, *Present Shock: When Everything Happens Now* (New York: Current, 2013), 72.

80. Van Grove, "Washington Post Launches Social Reader."

81. Facebook Developers, "Open Graph."

82. Facebook Developers.

83. Facebook Developers, "Publishing Permissions," https://developers .facebook.com/docs/publishing. Web page from 2012 is no longer available, and publish_stream no longer exists.

84. Mark Tonkelowitz, "Interesting News, Any Time You Visit," September 20, 2011, https://www.facebook.com/notes/facebook/interesting-news-any -time-you-visit/10150286921207131/.

85. Lessin, "Tell Your Story with Timeline."

86. Van Dijck, "Facebook and the Engineering of Connectivity," 145.

87. Van Dijck, 145.

88. Van Grove, "Washington Post Launches Social Reader."

89. John Herman, "Facebook Social Readers Are All Collapsing," *Buzz-Feed*, May 7, 2012, https://www.buzzfeed.com/jwherrman/facebook-social -readers-are-all-collapsing; Lauren Indvik, "Washington Post Moves Social Reader Off Facebook," *Mashable*, December 14, 2012, https://mashable .com/2012/12/14/washington-post-social-reader-off-facebook/.

90. Brittany Darwell, "Facebook's Frictionless Sharing Mistake," *Adweek*, January 22, 2013, http://www.adweek.com/digital/facebooks-frictionless -sharing-mistake/.

91. Darwell.

92. See a post on Facebook Help Community by Abby S. from the Facebook Help Team: https://www.facebook.com/help/community/question/?id =10210333738730902&answer_id=10210454701874905&rdrhc.

93. Kaldrack and Röhle, "Divide and Share."

94. Darwell, in "Facebook's Frictionless Sharing Mistake," claims that since September 2011, Facebook has not used the word "frictionless."

95. Facebook Developers, "Open Graph Stories," https://developers .facebook.com/docs/sharing/opengraph.

96. Kaldrack and Röhle, "Divide and Share."

97. Terranova, "Securing the Social," 122.

98. Tucker, "Douglas Rushkoff."

99. Ilana Gershon, "Un-friend My Heart: Facebook, Promiscuity and Heartbreak in a Neoliberal Age," *Anthropological Quarterly* 84, no. 4 (2011): 872.

100. Tucker, "Douglas Rushkoff."

101. Susanna Paasonen, "As Networks Fail: Affect, Technology, and the Notion of the User," *Television and New Media* 16, no. 8 (2015): 713.

Deactivate

1. Sean Dockray, "[iDC] Replacing Facebook (Geert Lovink)," May 28, 2010, https://lists.thing.net/pipermail/idc/2010-May/004284.html.

2. Félix Guattari, "Machinic Junkies," in *Soft Subversions: Texts and Interviews 1977–1985* (Los Angeles, Calif.: Semiotext(e), 2009), 158.

3. Guattari, 158.

4. Chun, *Updating to Remain the Same*, 6.

5. Cf. Maurizio Lazzarato, "The Machine," *Transversal* 10 (2006), http://www.eipcp.net/transversal/1106/lazzarato/en.

6. See also Mejias, "Limits of Networks as Models for Organizing the Social," 604.

7. Nigel Thrift, *Knowing Capitalism* (London: Sage, 2005), 7.

8. Cf. Gary Genosko, *Félix Guattari: A Critical Introduction* (London: Pluto Press, 2009), 92–93.

9. Genosko, 93.

10. Foucault, *Society Must Be Defended*.

11. Alexander Galloway and Eugene Thacker, *The Exploit: A Theory of Networks* (London: University of Minnesota Press, 2007).

12. Friedrich Kittler, "Thinking Colours and/or Machines," *Theory, Culture, and Society* 23, no. 7–8 (2006): 49.

13. One of the most famous pranks was a book called *Net.gener@tion,* which, to put it bluntly, was a book made of made-up content. As Tatiana Bazzichelli explained in *Networking: The Net as Artwork* (Aarhus, Denmark: Digital Aesthetics Research Center, 2008), this book was published in 1996 by Mondadori, one of Italy's biggest publishing houses, and taken off the market quickly when the Luther Blissett Project revealed the hoax (50).

14. Luther Blissett Project, "Seppuku!," September 6, 1999, http://www.lutherblissett.net/index_en.html.

15. Cory Arcangel, "friendster-suicide-live-in-person-dec-2005," *Cory Arcangel's Internet Portfolio Website and Portal* (blog), December 2005, http://www.coryarcangel.com/2005/12/friendster-suicide-live-in-person-dec-2005/.

16. Andrew Nunes, "'Delete Your Account' Unearths Our Awkward First-Times on Social Media," *The Creator's Project* (blog), September 9, 2015, http://thecreatorsproject.vice.com/en_uk/blog/delete-your-account-unearths-our-awkward-first-times-on-social-media.

17. Loretta Borelli, "The Suicide Irony: Seppuko and Web 2.0 Suicide Machine," *Digimac,* March 2010.

18. Man Bartlett, "Why I Deleted My Facebook Account," *Hyperallergic* (blog), July 10, 2012, http://hyperallergic.com/54018/man-bartlett-why-i-deleted-my-facebook-account/.

19. Nick Briz, *How to/Why Leave Facebook (on My Own Terms, without "Deleting" My Account),* accessed November 3, 2016, http://nickbriz.com/facebook/index.html.

20. Liam Scully, *A Digital Suicide,* a-n The Artists Information Company, March 17, 2015, https://www.a-n.co.uk/blogs/a-digital-suicide.

21. *Seppukoo.com,* http://www.seppukoo.com/.

22. *Web 2.0 Suicide Machine,* http://suicidemachine.org/.

23. Les Liens Invisibles, "About," accessed December 19, 2016, http://www.lesliensinvisibles.org/about/.

24. Moddr_, "Moddr_?," accessed December 19, 2016, http://moddr.net/moddr_?.

25. *Seppukoo.com,* "Re: Cease and Desist Violating Facebook's Statement of Rights and Responsibilities," December 16, 2009, http://www.seppukoo.com/docs/seppukoo_cease_desist.pdf.

26. *Web 2.0 Suicide Machine,* "Re: Cease and Desist Violating Facebook's Statement of Rights and Responsibilities," January 6, 2010, http://www.suicidemachine.org/download/Web_2.0_Suicide_Machine.pdf.

27. This information is based on the cease-and-desist letters published on the *Web 2.0 Suicide Machine* and *Seppukoo.com* websites.

28. Despite the cease-and-desist letters, *Web 2.0 Suicide Machine* and *Seppukoo.com* tried to keep up and running for a while. However, in February 2011, *Seppukoo.com* notified that, "due to the paradoxical controversy between the giant Facebook and Seppukoo, our suicidal services are now useless." Equally, *Web 2.0 Suicide Machine* no longer works. The disturbance these art projects created for Facebook was temporary. What is important here, however, is the way they illustrated the mechanisms and ideologies behind Facebook and digital capitalism in general.

29. Jussi Parikka, "Ethologies of Software Art: What Can a Digital Body of Code Do?," in *Deleuze and Contemporary Art,* ed. Stephen Zepke and Simon O'Sullivan (Edinburgh: Edinburgh University Press, 2010), 116.

30. Jussi Parikka and Tony D. Sampson, "Anomalous Objects and Digital Culture," in *The Spam Book,* ed. Jussi Parikka and Tony D. Sampson (Cresskill, N.J.: Hampton Press, 2009), 11.

31. Matthew Fuller and Andrew Goffey, "Towards an Evil Media Studies," in Parikka and Sampson, *Spam Book,* 141.

32. Parikka and Sampson, "Anomalous Objects and Digital Culture," 11.

33. Galloway and Thacker, *Exploit,* 70.

34. Galloway and Thacker.

35. Foucault, *Society Must Be Defended,* 245.

36. Foucault.

37. Cf. John Durham Peters, who, in *The Marvelous Clouds: Toward a Philosophy of Elemental Media* (Chicago: University of Chicago Press, 2015), states, "The old idea that media are environments can be flipped: environments are also media" (3).

38. Galloway and Thacker, *Exploit,* 70; Parikka, "Ethologies of Software Art," 116.

39. Foucault, *Security, Territory, Population,* 21

40. Foucault, *Society Must Be Defended,* 246.

41. Galloway and Thacker, *Exploit,* 72. Original emphasis removed by the author.

42. Van Dijck, "Users Like You?," 47.

43. Scully, "A Digital Suicide."

44. Facebook, "Data Policy," last modified September 29, 2016, https://www.facebook.com/full_data_use_policy.

45. Facebook.

46. Facebook.

47. Van Dijck, "Users Like You?," 47, 51, 53.

48. Cf. Dimitry Kleiner and Brian Wyrick, "InfoEnclosure," in *Proud to Be Flesh: A Mute Magazine Anthology of Cultural Politics after the Net,* ed. Josephine Berry Slater and Pauline van Mourik Broekman (London: Mute, 2009), 5.

49. Kleiner and Wyrick, 3.

50. Mejias, "Limits of Networks as Models for Organizing the Social," 607.

51. F-Secure, "How to Save Face: 6 Tips for Safer Facebooking," August 5, 2010, https://safeandsavvy.f-secure.com/2010/08/05/protect-yourself-facebook/.

52. Jussi Parikka, "Digital Monsters, Binary Aliens: Computer Viruses, Capitalism, and the Flow of Information," *Fibreculture,* no. 4 (2006), http://four.fibreculturejournal.org/fcj-019-digital-monsters-binary-aliens-%E2%80%93-computer-viruses-capitalism-and-the-flow-of-information/; Tony Sampson, "The Accidental Topology of Digital Culture: How the Network Becomes Viral," *Transformations,* no. 14 (2007), http://www.transformationsjournal.org/journal/issue_14/article_05.shtml.

53. Bucher, "Want to Be on the Top?"

54. Foucault, *Society Must Be Defended,* 249.

55. Richard Grusin, *Premediation: Affect and Mediality after 9/11* (London: Palgrave Macmillan, 2010).

56. Grusin, 48.

57. Portwood-Stacer, "Media Refusal and Conspicuous Non-consumption."

58. Light and Cassidy, "Strategies for the Suspension and Prevention of Connection," 1179.

59. Facebook, "Deactivating and Deleting Accounts," accessed October 20, 2016, https://www.facebook.com/help/359046244166395/.

60. Facebook.

61. Grusin, *Premediation*, 46.

62. David Savat, "Deleuze's Objectile: From Discipline to Modulation," in *Deleuze and New Technology,* ed. Mark Poster and David Savat (Edinburgh: Edinburgh University Press, 2009), 57.

63. Savat, 52–53.

64. Gilles Deleuze, "Postscript on the Societies of Control," *October 59* (Winter 1992): 5. See also chapter 1 in this book. Furthermore, being a dividual is a philosophical concept, but it is also a trope that can be traced in popular culture. For example, episode 4 of season 14 of *South Park* shows how one of the main characters, Stan Marsh, is literally drawn inside the world of Facebook and needs to fight against his own Facebook profile.

65. Genosko, *Félix Guattari,* 101.

66. Rita Raley, *Tactical Media* (Minneapolis: University of Minnesota Press, 2009), 3–4.

67. Raley, 6.

68. Bartlett, "Why I Deleted My Facebook Account."

69. *Seppukoo.com,* "About," accessed December 19, 2016, http://www.seppukoo.com/about.

70. *Web 2.0 Suicide Machine,* "About," accessed April 27, 2016, http://www.suicidemachine.org/.

71. Galloway and Thacker, *Exploit,* 81.

72. Raley, *Tactical Media,* 12.

73. Parikka, "Ethologies of Software Art," 118.

74. Félix Guattari, *Chaosmosis—an Ethico-Aesthetic Paradigm* (Bloomington: Indiana University Press, 1995), 49.

75. Gilles Deleuze, "Postscript on Control Societies," in *Negotiations,* 180.

76. Raley, *Tactical Media,* 12.

77. Dockray, "[iDC] Replacing Facebook (Geert Lovink)."

78. Dockray.

79. Dockray.

80. Raley, *Tactical Media,* 25.

81. Raley, 25–26.

82. Deleuze, *Difference and Repetition,* 137–38.

83. Seppukoo.com, "About."

84. Galloway and Thacker, *Exploit,* 135–36.

85. This group no longer exists online.

86. Terranova, *Network Culture,* 136.

87. Herman Melville, "Bartleby the Scrivener, a Story of Wall Street (Part 1)," *Putnam's Monthly Magazine of American Literature, Science, and Art* 0002, no. 11 (November 1853); Melville, "Bartleby the Scrivener, a Story of

Wall Street (Part 2)," *Putnam's Monthly Magazine of American Literature, Science, and Art* 0002, no. 12 (December 1853).

88. Gilles Deleuze, "Bartleby; or, the Formula," in *Essays Critical and Clinical* (London: Verso, 1998), 70–71; Raley, *Tactical Media,* 25.

89. Michael Hardt and Antonio Negri, *Multitude: War and Democracy in the Age of Empire* (New York: Penguin Books, 2004), 58.

90. Mejias, "Limits of Networks as Models for Organizing the Social," 612, 614.

91. Dockray, "[iDC] Replacing Facebook (Geert Lovink)."

92. Parikka, "Ethologies of Software Art," 119.

Die

1. Facebook, "What Is a Legacy Contact and What Can They Do?," https://www.facebook.com/help/1568013990080948?helpref=faq_content.

2. George Harrison, "Online Graveyard: How Social Media Companies Keeping Up Dead People's Profiles Makes It Impossible for Relatives to Deal with Grief—with 50 Million on Facebook Alone," *Sun,* January 16, 2018, https://www.thesun.co.uk/tech/5317765/social-media-dead-peoples-profiles/.

3. Kristen V. Brown, "We Calculated the Year Dead People on Facebook Could Outnumber the Living," Fusion.net, March 4, 2016, http://fusion.net/story/276237/the-number-of-dead-people-on-facebook-will-soon-outnumber-the-living/.

4. Bjorn Nansen, Tamara Kohn, Michael Arnold, Luke van Ryn, and Martin Gibbs, "Social Media in the Funeral Industry: On the Digitization of Grief," *Journal of Broadcasting and Electronic Media* 61, no. 1 (2017): 75.

5. Tiziana Terranova, "Futurepublic: On Information Warfare, Bio-racism and Hegemony as Noopolitics," *Theory, Culture, and Society* 24, no. 3 (2007): 126.

6. Bruno Latour and Vincent Antonin Lépinay, *The Science of Passionate Interests: An Introduction to Gabriel Tarde's Economic Anthropology* (Chicago: Prickly Paradigm Press, 2009), 8.

7. Jed Brubaker, Funda Kivran-Swaine, Lee Taber, and Gillian R. Hayes, "Grief-Stricken in a Crowd: The Language of Bereavement and Distress in Social Media," paper presented at the 6th International AAAI Conference on Weblogs and Social Media, 2011, accessed April 15, 2013, http://www.aaai.org/ocs/index.php/ICWSM/ICWSM12/paper/view/4622.

8. Nancy Baym, *Personal Connections in the Digital Age* (Cambridge: Polity Press, 2010), 134.

9. Jed Brubaker and Gillian R. Hayes, "'We Will Never Forget You

[Online]': An Empirical Investigation of Post-Mortem MySpace Comments," paper presented at the ACM Conference on Computer Supported Cooperative Work, 2011, http://dl.acm.org/citation.cfm?id=1958843.

10. Rebecca Kern, Abbe Forman, and Gisela Gil-Equi, "R.I.P.: Remain in Perpetuity—Facebook Memorial Pages," *Telematics and Informatics* 30 (2013): 3, http://www.sciencedirect.com/science/article/pii/S0736585312000263.

11. Alice Marwick and Nicole B. Ellison "'There Isn't Wifi in Heaven!' Negotiating Visibility on Facebook Memorial Pages," *Journal of Broadcasting and Electronic Media* 56, no. 3 (2012): 378–400.

12. Marwick and Ellison, 379.

13. Schäfer, *Bastard Culture!*, 51.

14. Andreas Kaplan and Michael Haenlein, "Users of the World, Unite! The Challenges and Opportunities of Social Media," *Business Horizons* 53, no. 1 (2010): 61.

15. Mark Andrejevic, "Privacy, Exploitation, and the Digital Enclosure," *Amsterdam Law Forum* 1, no. 4 (2009), http://ojs.ubvu.vu.nl/alf/article/view /94/168.

16. Tarleton Gillespie, "The Politics of 'Platforms,'" *New Media and Society* 12, no. 3 (2010): 359.

17. Marwick and Ellison, "'There Isn't Wifi in Heaven!,'" 380.

18. Brubaker and Hayes, "We Will Never Forget You [Online]."

19. Jacques Derrida, "I'll Have to Wander All Alone," in *The Work of Mourning* (Chicago: Chicago University Press, 2001), 193.

20. Anna Munster, "From a Biopolitical 'Will to Life' to a Noopolitical Ethos of Death in the Aesthetics of Digital Code," *Theory, Culture, and Society* 28, no. 6 (2011): 69.

21. Max Kelly, "Memories of Friends Departed Endure on Facebook," *Facebook Blog,* October 6, 2009, https://blog.facebook.com/blog.php?post =163091042130; Facebook, "Remembering Loved Ones on Facebook," December 7, 2011, https://www.facebook.com/notes/facebook-safety/remembering -loved-ones-on-facebook/306746312679491.

22. In this chapter, the research materials consist of Facebook documents dated between the years 2012 and 2013, which followed the introduction of Facebook's dead user policy. Facebook, "How Do I Report a Deceased User or an Account That Needs to Be Memorialized?," https://www .facebook.com/help/?faq=150486848354038&in_context; Facebook, "How Do I Submit a Special Request for a Deceased User's Account on the Site?," https://www.facebook.com/help/?faq=265593773453448; Facebook, "Report a Deceased Person's Profile," https://www.facebook.com/help/contact/?id= 305593649477238; Facebook, "Memorialization Request," https://www.face book.com/help/contact/305593649477238?rdrhc; Facebook, "What Happens

When a Deceased Person's Account Is Memorialized?," https://www.facebook
.com/help/359046244166395/.

23. Kelly, "Memories of Friends Departed Endure on Facebook."

24. Friedrich Kittler, *Gramophone, Film, Typewriter* (Stanford, Calif.:
Stanford University Press, 1999), xxxix.

25. Geoffrey Winthrop-Young, *Kittler and the Media* (Cambridge: Polity
Press, 2011), 65.

26. Foucault, *Society Must Be Defended.*

27. Maurizio Lazzarato, "Neoliberalism in Action: Inequality, Insecurity
and the Reconstitution of the Social," *Theory, Culture, and Society* 26, no. 6
(2009): 112.

28. Tiziana Terranova, "Another Life: The Nature of Political Economy in
Foucault's Genealogy of Biopolitics," *Theory, Culture, and Society* 26, no. 6
(2009): 240.

29. John Cheney-Lippold, "A New Algorithmic Identity: Soft Biopolitics and the Modulation of Control," *Theory, Culture, and Society* 28, no. 6
(2011): 164–81.

30. Foucault, *Society Must Be Defended,* 247–48.

31. Kelly, "Memories of Friends Departed Endure on Facebook."

32. Whitney Phillips, "LOLing at Tragedy: Facebook Trolls, Memorial
Pages and Resistance to Grief Online," *First Monday* 16, no. 12 (2011), http://
firstmonday.org/htbin/cgiwrap/bin/ojs/index.php/fm/article/view/3168/3115.

33. Facebook, "How Do I Submit a Special Request?"

34. Facebook.

35. Facebook, "How Do I Report a Deceased User?"

36. Facebook, "Memorialization Request."

37. Kelly, "Memories of Friends Departed Endure on Facebook."

38. Phillips, "LOLing at Tragedy."

39. Facebook, "Remembering Loved Ones on Facebook," December 7, 2011,
https://www.facebook.com/notes/facebook-safety/remembering-loved
-ones-on-facebook/306746312679491.

40. Facebook, "What Will Happen to My Facebook Account If I Pass Away?,"
https://www.facebook.com/help/103897939701143?helpref=faq_content.

41. Foucault, *Society Must Be Defended,* 248.

42. Facebook, "Remembering Loved Ones on Facebook."

43. Maurizio Lazzarato, "The Concepts of Life and Living in the Societies
of Control," in *Deleuze and the Social,* ed. Martin Fuglsang and Bent Meier
Sorensen, 179-190 (Edinburgh: Edinburgh University Press, 2006), 86.

44. Kern et al., "R.I.P.," 3.

45. Lazzarato, "Concepts of Life and Living", 85; see also Robert W. Gehl,
"What's on Your Mind? Social Media Monopolies and Noopower," *First*

Monday 18, no. 3–4 (2013), http://firstmonday.org/ojs/index.php/fm/article/view/4618/3421.

46. Terranova, "Futurepublic," 140.

47. Facebook, "Remembering Loved Ones on Facebook."

48. Light and Cassidy, "Strategies for the Suspension and Prevention of Connection," 1179.

49. Kern et al., "R.I.P.," 3.

50. Brubaker and Hayes, "We Will Never Forget You [Online]," 129.

51. With this assertion, Gehl, in "What's on Your Mind?," wants to address that social media sites like Facebook want to control what is on our minds, and the capability to do this is based on technologies that effectively mediate the message and are capable of spreading it.

52. For more information about the project, see http://www.warveterans.be/generalites/about-us/id-menu-443, accessed December 20, 2016.

53. Marwick and Ellison, "'There Isn't Wifi in Heaven!'"

54. Marwick and Ellison, 395.

55. Lazzarato, in "Concepts of Life and Living," is referring to a very particular understanding of memory emerging in the thought of Friedrich Nietzsche, Henri Bergson, and Gabriel Tarde; he argues that memory needs to be considered an active operation where the virtual is actualized (184–85).

56. Lazzarato, 184.

57. Bruno Latour, Pablo Jensen, Tomasso Venturini, Sébastian Grauwin, and Dominique Boullier, "The Whole Is Always Smaller Than Its Parts: A Digital Test of Gabriel Tarde's Monads," *British Journal of Sociology* 64, no. 4 (2012): 593.

58. Latour et al., 598.

59. Latour et al., 599.

60. Latour et al., 599.

61. Latour and Lépinay, *Science of Passionate Interests,* 8.

62. Scott Lash and Celia Lury, *Global Culture Industry: The Mediation of Things* (Cambridge: Polity Press, 2007), 8.

63. Lash and Lury, *Global Culture Industry,* 8.

64. Tama Leaver, "The Social Media Contradiction: Data Mining and Digital Death," *MC Journal* 16, no. 2 (2013), http://journal.media-culture.org.au/index.php/mcjournal/article/viewArticle/625.

Disconnect

1. Dan Yoder, "10 Reasons to Delete Your Facebook Account," *Business Insider,* May 3, 2010, http://www.businessinsider.com/10-reasons-to-delete-your-facebook-account-2010-5.

2. Gilles Deleuze and Félix Guattari, *What Is Philosophy?* (New York: Columbia University Press, 1994), 16.

3. *Oxford Living Dictionaries,* s.v. "disconnect," https://en.oxford dictionaries.com/definition/disconnect.

4. Cf. Van Dijck, *Culture of Connectivity,* 13.

5. Quit Facebook Day, "We Are Quitting Facebook," http://www.quit facebookday.com/.

6. Diaspora Foundation, "Diaspora Means a Brighter Future for All of Us," September 21, 2011, accessed via the WaybackMachine October 14, 2016, http://blog.diasporafoundation.org/2011/09/21/diaspora-means-a-brighter -future-for-all-of-us.html.

7. Gail Sullivan, "Social Network Ello Gets Boost after Facebook Boots Drag Queens," *Washington Post,* September 25, 2014, https://www.wash ingtonpost.com/news/morning-mix/wp/2014/09/25/social-network-ello-gets -boost-after-facebook-boots-drag-queens/?utm_term=.826c268a36f6.

8. Ello, "Ello Manifesto," July 3, 2014, https://ello.co/wtf/about/ello -manifesto.

9. If we compare Facebook's protocols to alternative social media sites like Diaspora*, we see two different systems of connection: centralized and decentralized. Facebook is a centralized platform, where the company owns not only the data users contribute but also the infrastructure, such as the servers through which data run and are stored. On Diaspora*, user data go through local servers that can be set up anywhere. Diaspora* claims that through its decentralized architecture, it can provide more freedom to users to do what they want and also control their privacy.

10. O'Reilly, "What Is Web 2.0."

11. Terranova, *Network Culture.*

12. Terranova, 48.

13. Terranova, 48.

14. Hardt and Negri, *Multitude,* 65.

15. Franco "Bifo" Berardi, *The Soul at Work: From Alienation to Autonomy* (Los Angeles, Calif.: Semiotext(e), 2009), 98–105.

16. Chun, *Control and Freedom,* 3.

17. Nicole S. Cohen, "The Valorization of Surveillance: Towards a Political Economy of Facebook," *Democratic Communiqué* 22, no. 1 (2008): 11–12.

18. James Vincent, "Former Facebook Exec Says Social Media Is Ripping Apart Society," *The Verge,* December 11, 2017, https://www.theverge .com/2017/12/11/16761016/former-facebook-exec-ripping-apart-society.

19. Vincent.

20. Digital Detox, "Hurry Up and Slow Down," accessed February 3, 2016, http://digitaldetox.org/about/.

21. Digital Detox, "Digital Detox Retreats," accessed February 3, 2016, http://digitaldetox.org/retreats/.

22. Portwood-Stacer, "Media Refusal and Conspicuous Non-consumption," 1054.

23. Portwood-Stacer, 1048, 1051.

24. Portwood-Stacer, 1053–54.

25. Van Dijck, *Culture of Connectivity,* 51.

26. Light, *Disconnecting with Social Networking Sites,* 151.

27. Light, 101–2.

28. Jussi Parikka, *Digital Contagions: A Media Archaeology of Computer Viruses* (New York: Peter Lang, 2007), 18.

29. Tarleton Gillespie, "The Politics of 'Platforms,'" *New Media and Society* 12, no. 3 (2010): 350.

30. Langlois, "Participatory Culture and the New Governance of Communication."

31. Alex Stamos, "An Update on Information Operations on Facebook," Facebook Newsroom, September 6, 2017, https://newsroom.fb.com/news/2017/09/information-operations-update/.

32. Stamos.

33. For a discussion of connection strategies, see Nicole B. Ellison, Charles Steinfield, and Cliff Lampe, "Connection Strategies: Social Capital Implications of Facebook-Enabled Communication Practices," *New Media and Society* 13, no. 6 (2010): 888–89.

34. See for example, Twitter, "Announcing the Twitter Ads API," February 20, 2013, https://blog.twitter.com/2013/announcing-the-twitter-ads-api; Twitter, "Celebrating 3 Years of Twitter Ads API Innovation," *Twitter Blog,* March 1, 2016, accessed October 24, 2016, https://blog.twitter.com/2016/celebrating-3-years-of-twitter-ads-api-innovation.

35. Bucher, "Objects of Intense Feeling."

36. Kate Crawford, "Can an Algorithm Be Agonistic? Ten Scenes from Life in Calculated Publics," *Science, Technology, and Human Values* 41, no. 1 (2016): 79.

37. Paul Lewis, "'Our Minds Can Be Hijacked': The Tech Insiders Who Fear a Smartphone Dystopia," *Guardian,* October 6, 2017, https://www.theguardian.com/technology/2017/oct/05/smartphone-addiction-silicon-valley-dystopia.

38. Lewis.

39. Lewis.

40. Gilles Deleuze and Claire Parnet, *Dialogues II* (London: Continuum, 2006), 322.

41. As Gilles Deleuze argues in *Two Regimes of Madness: Texts and Interviews 1975–1995* (Cambridge, Mass.: Semiotext(e), 2007), "control is not discipline. You do not confine people with a highway. But by making highways,

you multiply the means of control. I am not saying this is the only aim of highways, but people can travel infinitely and 'freely' without being confined while being perfectly controlled. That is our future" (322).

42. Raiford Guins, *Edited Clean Version: Technology and the Culture of Control* (Minneapolis: University of Minnesota Press, 2009), 21.

43. Guins, *Edited Clean Version,* 15–23.

44. Melissa Gregg, "Getting Things Done: Productivity, Self-Management, and the Order of Things," in *Networked Affect,* ed. Ken Hillis, Susanna Paasonen, and Michael Petit (Cambridge, Mass.: MIT Press, 2015), 188.

45. Patricia Clough, *The Affective Turn: Theorizing the Social* (Durham, N.C.: Duke University Press, 2007), 27.

46. Lewis, "Our Minds Can Be Hijacked."

47. Lewis.

48. Lewis.

49. Massumi, "Principle of Unrest," 14.

50. Kramer et al., "Experimental Evidence of Massive-Scale Emotional Contagion."

51. Kramer et al., 8788.

52. Kramer et al., 8788.

53. Inder M. Verma, "Editorial Expression of Concern: Experimental Evidence of Massivescale Emotional Contagion through Social Networks," *Proceedings of the National Academy of Sciences of the United States of America* 111, no. 29 (2013): 10779.

54. Grusin, *Premediation,* 79.

55. Gregory J. Seigworth and Melissa Gregg, "An Inventory of Shimmers," in *The Affect Theory Reader,* ed. Melissa Gregg and Gregory J. Seigworth, 5–8 (Durham, N.C.: Duke University Press, 2010).

56. Ruth Leys, "The Turn to Affect: A Critique," *Critical Inquiry* 37 (Spring 2011): 438.

57. Clare Hemmings, "Invoking Affect: Cultural Theory and the Ontological Turn," *Cultural Studies* 19, no. 5 (2005): 552.

58. Brian Massumi, interview by Mary Zournazi, accessed June 11, 2013, http://www.international-festival.org/node/111.

59. Massumi, *Parables for the Virtual,* 37–38.

60. Deleuze, *Spinoza,* 19.

61. Massumi, "Principle of Unrest," 14.

62. Zuckerberg, referenced in David Kirkpatrick, *The Facebook Effect: The Inside Story of the Company That Is Connecting the World* (New York: Simon and Schuster, 2011), 217.

63. Paasonen et al., "Introduction," 1.

64. Cf. Paasonen, *Carnal Resonance,* 258.

65. Bucher, "Friendship Assemblage."

66. Twitter, "About Your Twitter Timeline," accessed October 24, 2016, https://support.twitter.com/articles/164083.

67. Kramer et al., "Experimental Evidence of Massive-Scale Emotional Contagion."

68. Paasonen et al., "Introduction," 3; Mona Mannevuo, *Affektitehdas: Työn rationalisoinnin historiallisia jatkumoita* (Turku: Annales Universitatis Turkuensis, 2015), 195.

69. Paasonen, "As Networks Fail," 13

70. Terranova, *Network Culture,* 19.

71. Zizi Papacharissi, *Affective Publics: Sentiment, Technology, and Politics* (New York: Oxford University Press, 2014), 26.

72. Paasonen, "As Networks Fail," 3.

73. Mark Coté, "Technics and the Human Sensorium: Rethinking Media Theory through the Body," *Theory and Event* 14, no. 4 (2010), https://muse.jhu.edu/article/407142.

74. Jenkins et al., *Spreadable Media,* 57.

75. Robert W. Gehl, "What's on Your Mind? Social Media Monopolies and Noopower," *First Monday* 18, no. 3–4 (2013), http://www.uic.edu/htbin/cgiwrap/bin/ojs/index.php/fm/article/view/4618/3421.

76. Light and Cassidy, "Strategies for the Suspension and Prevention of Connection," 1171.

77. Light and Cassidy, 1169.

78. Light and Cassidy, 1180.

79. Grusin, *Premediation.* See also chapter 3.

80. Richard Grusin, "Premediation and the Virtual Occupation of Wall Street," *Theory and Event* 14, no. 4 (Suppl.) (2011).

81. Grusin, *Premediation,* 12.

82. As former president of the United States George W. Bush phrased it, as quoted in Brian Massumi, "The Remains of the Day," in *Emotions, Politics, and War,* ed. Linda Åhäll and Thomas Gregory (London: Routledge, 2015), 18, "if we wait for threats to fully materialize, we will have waited too long. We must take the battle to the enemy, disrupt his plans and confront the worst threats before they emerge. In the world we have entered, the only path to safety is the path to action." See also Brian Massumi, "Potential Politics and the Primacy of Preemption," *Theory and Event* 10, no. 2 (2007).

83. Massumi, "Remains of the Day," 19.

84. Mark Andrejevic, "The Work That Affective Economics Does," *Cultural Studies* 25, no. 4–5 (2011): 614.

85. Frank Pasquale, *The Black Box Society: The Secret Algorithms That Control Money and Information* (Cambridge, Mass.: Harvard University Press, 2015).

86. Safiya Umoja Noble, "Google Search: Hyper-visibility as a Means

of Rendering Black Women and Girls Invisible," *InVisibile Culture*, no. 19 (2013).

87. Tucker, "Douglas Rushkoff."

88. Portwood-Stacers, "Media Refusal and Conspicuous Non-consumption," 1047.

89. Kirkpatrick, *Facebook Effect*, 275.

90. Kirkpatrick, 275–76.

91. Pingdom, in a blog post "How Many Sites Have Facebook Integration? You'd Be Surprised," *Pingdom Tech Blog*, June 18, 2012, accessed June 11, 2013, http://royal.pingdom.com/2012/06/18/how-many-sites-have-facebook-integration-youd-be-surprised/, explains that the research was done by analyzing the HTML code of the ten thousand websites ranked by Alexa, the web information company. While the research method is not explained in sufficient detail to evaluate the exact validity of the results, and this research is already several years old, one can nevertheless draw rough conclusions that Facebook is widely integrated with different websites and services.

92. Light and Cassidy, "Strategies for the Suspension and Prevention of Connection," 1181.

93. Terranova, "Securing the Social," 114. See also chapter 1 in this book.

94. Terranova, 114.

95. One of the culminations of Facebook's mission statement to "make the world more open and connected" was in 2011, when it was revealed that Facebook was also tracking nonusers who had merely visited the main site. When the user accessed Facebook.com, a cookie was installed on her computer. This cookie was then able to track Facebook users and nonusers who visited pages that had Facebook integrations, such as a Like button or other installed Facebook plug-ins. According to Facebook, this was not intentional but was caused by a bug in the programming and has now been removed. See Suw Charman-Anderson, "Facebook Finally Admits to Tracking Non-Users," *Tech2* (blog), November 17, 2011, http://www.firstpost.com/tech/facebook-finally-admits-to-tracking-non-users-133684.html.

96. Zuckerberg's letter to prospective investors highlights Facebook's future plans for connectivity as a humanitarian project: "There is a huge need and a huge opportunity to get everyone in the world connected, to give everyone a voice and to help transform society for the future. The scale of the technology and infrastructure that must be built is unprecedented, and we believe this is the most important problem we can focus on." Facebook Inc., "Form S-1," 67.

97. Grusin, *Premediation*, 128.

98. Manuel Castells, *Networks of Outrage and Hope: Social Movements in the Internet Age* (Cambridge: Polity Press, 2015), 63.

99. Philip N. Howard, Aiden Duffy, Deen Freelon, Muzammil Hussain,

Will Mari, and Marwa Mazaid, "Opening Closed Regimes: What Was the Role of Social Media during the Arab Spring?" (working paper, Project on Information Technology and Political Islam, 2011), 2.

100. Philip N. Howard, Sheetal D. Agarwal, and Muzammil M. Hussain, "When Do States Disconnect Their Digital Networks? Regime Responses to the Political Uses of Social Media," *The Communication Review* 14, no. 3 (2011): 216–32.

101. Paasonen, "As Networks Fail," 6.

102. Castells, *Networks of Outrage and Hope,* 64.

103. Howard et al., "When Do States Disconnect Their Digital Networks?," 11.

104. Cf. Ronald J. Deibert, "Dark Guests and Great Firewalls: The Internet and Chinese Security Policy," *Journal of Social Issues* 58, no. 1 (2002): 147.

105. Castells, *Networks of Outrage and Hope,* 63.

106. Massumi, "Principles of Unrest," 11.

107. Castells, 66.

Log Out

1. Emily Steel and Geoffrey Fowler, "Facebook in Privacy Breach: Top-Ranked Applications Transmit Personal IDs, a Journal Investigation Finds," *Wall Street Journal,* October 18, 2010, http://www.wsj.com/articles/SB10001 424052702304772804575558484075236968.

2. Steel and Fowler.

3. Steel and Fowler.

4. Chun, *Updating to Remain the Same,* 12.

5. Chun, 13.

6. Chun, 172.

7. Disconnect, https://disconnect.me/.

8. Klint Finley, "Out in the Open: Ex-Google Ad Man Saves You from Ad Hell," *Wired,* December 23, 2013, https://www.wired.com/2013/12/disconnect/.

9. Zack Whittaker, "Comcast Wants Its Broadband Users to Pay for Their Privacy," Zdnet.com, August 3, 2016, http://www.zdnet.com/article/comcast-wants-its-broadband-users-to-pay-for-their-privacy/.

10. Chun, *Updating to Remain the Same,* 10.

11. Steven Shaviro, *Connected, or What It Means to Live in the Network Society* (Minneapolis: University of Minnesota Press, 2003), 3.

12. Alison Hearn, "Structuring Feeling: Web 2.0, Online Ranking and Rating, and the Digital 'Reputation' Economy," *ephemera: Theory and Politics in Organization* 10, no. 3/4 (2010): 428.

13. Chun, *Updating to Remain the Same,* 23.

14. "Life Event," Facebook, https://www.facebook.com/help/1378299 36332495.

15. Sari Östman, "Life Publishing on the Internet—a Playful Field of Life-Narrating," in *The Digital Turn: User's Practices and Cultural Transformations,* ed. Runnel Pille, Pruulmann-Vengerfeldt Pille, Viires Piret, and Laak Marin (Bern, Switzerland: Peter Lang, 2013), 147–48.

16. Maurizio Lazzaratto, "Neoliberalism in Action: Inequality, Insecurity and the Reconstitution of the Social," *Theory, Culture, and Society* 26, no. 6 (2009): 111.

17. See Bucher, "Want to Be on the Top?," 1168.

18. Galloway, *Interface Effect,* 137.

19. Facebook, "Easier, More Effective Ways to Reach the Right People on Facebook," February 20, 2016, https://www.facebook.com/business/news/Core-Audiences.

20. Coté and Pybus, "Learning to Immaterial Labour 2.0," 90, 96.

21. Galloway, *Interface Effect,* 137.

22. Cheney-Lippold, "A New Algorithmic Identity," 165.

23. Amoore, *Politics of Possibility,* 50.

24. Cheney-Lippold, "A New Algorithmic Identity," 165.

25. Cheney-Lippold, 177–78.

26. Facebook, "Accessing Your Facebook Data," https://www.facebook .com/help/405183566203254.

27. Louise Amoore, "Data Derivatives: On the Emergence of a Security Risk Calculus for Our Times," *Theory, Culture, and Society* 28, no. 6 (2011): 24–43.

28. Amoore, 28.

29. Amoore, 28.

30. Cade Metz, "How Facebook Knows When Its Ads Influence Your Off-line Purchases," *Wired,* November 12, 2014, http://www.wired.com/2014/12/facebook-knows-ads-influence-offline-purchases/.

31. Amoore, *Politics of Possibility,* 42.

32. Tero Karppi and Kate Crawford, "Social Media, Financial Algorithms and the Hack Crash," *Theory, Culture, and Society* 33, no. 1 (2015): 73–92.

33. Arvidsson, "Facebook and Finance," 4.

34. In *Updating to Remain the Same,* Chun discusses the notion of habit through, for example, the writings of Gilles Deleuze, Henri Bergson, and Gabriel Tarde and connects it to the modes of neoliberal control and finds it as a key element behind our social media connectivity.

35. Chun, 2.

36. Chun, 54.

37. Deleuze, *Difference and Repetition,* 263.

38. Amoore, *Politics of Possibility,* 7.

39. Van Dijck, *Culture of Connectivity*, 174–75.

40. Deleuze, *Difference and Repetition*, 56.

41. Luciana Parisi, *Contagious Architecture: Computation, Aesthetics, and Space* (Cambridge, Mass.: MIT Press, 2013), 263.

42. Deleuze, *Difference and Repetition*, 57.

43. Daniel W. Smith, *Essays on Deleuze* (Edinburgh: Edinburgh University Press, 2012), 246.

44. Smith.

45. Andrew Culp, *Dark Deleuze* (Minneapolis: University of Minnesota Press, 2016), 66.

46. Gilles Deleuze, *Cinema 2: The Time-Image* (London: Athlone Press, 2000), 280.

47. Massumi, *Parables for the Virtual*, 25.

48. "About," Commodify.Us, http://commodify.us/about; Marc Garrett, "Commodify.Us: Our Data Our Terms," November 8, 2013, http://www.furtherfield.org/features/reviews/commodify-us-our-data-our-terms.

49. "About," http://commodify.us/.

50. "Howto," Commodify.Us, http://commodify.us/#howto.

51. Garrett, "Commodify.Us."

52. Chun, *Updating to Remain the Same*, 172.

53. Culp, *Dark Deleuze*, 8, 66.

54. Culp, 65–66.

55. Culp, 65–66.

56. Regina Dungan's public F8 talk quoted in Olivia Solon, "Facebook Has 60 People Working on How to Read Your Mind," *Guardian*, April 19, 2017, https://www.theguardian.com/technology/2017/apr/19/facebook-mind-reading-technology-f8.

57. Solon, "Facebook Has 60 People."

58. "Brain–Computer Interface Engineer, Building 8," Facebook, https://www.facebook.com/careers/jobs/a0I1200000JXqeWEAT/; Josh Constine, "Facebook Is Building Brain–Computer Interfaces for Typing and Skin-Hearing," April 19, 2017, https://techcrunch.com/2017/04/19/facebook-brain-interface/.

59. Dungan, as quoted in Constine, "Facebook Is Building Brain–Computer Interfaces."

60. Constine, "Facebook Is Building Brain–Computer Interfaces."

61. Friedrich Kittler, "The History of Communication Media," *CTheory*, no. 114 (July 30, 1996).

62. Kittler.

63. Cf. Sampson, *The Assemblage Brain*.

64. Deleuze and Guattari, *What Is Philosophy?*, 59.

65. Deleuze and Guattari, 60.

Index

TERO KARPPI is assistant professor in the Institute of Communication, Culture, Information, and Technology and in the Faculty of Information at the University of Toronto.

CPSIA information can be obtained
at www.ICGtesting.com
Printed in the USA
BVHW090030231218
536229BV00012BA/93/P